HOW TO HUG A
Hedgehog

HOW TO HUG A
Hedgehog

12 Keys for

Connecting

with

Teens

BRAD WILCOX AND JERRICK ROBBINS

FAMILIUS

FAMILIUS

Published by Familius LLC, www.familius.com
Familius books are available at special discounts for bulk purchases for sales promotions, family, or corporate use. Special editions, including personalized covers, excerpts of existing books, or books with corporate logos, can be created in large quantities for special needs. For more information, contact Premium Sales at 559-876-2170 or email specialmarkets@familius.com

Library of Congress Catalog-in-Publication Data
2014948316

pISBN 978-1-939629-19-7
eISBN 978-1-939629-89-0
Printed in the United States of America

Edited by Brooke Jorden
Cover Design by David Miles
Book Design by Brooke Jorden

10 9 8 7 6 5 4 3 2 1

First Edition

Acknowledgments

It has been a wonderful experience writing this book, and we are grateful for all who have made this possible. Our friends at Familius are superb. We would especially like to thank Christopher Robbins, Maggie Wickes, Brooke Jorden, David Miles, and the rest of their tremendous team for the many hours they've spent designing, editing, and preparing this book for publication.

Special thanks go out to the individuals who have allowed us to share their stories and experiences. We have learned so much from them and appreciate their examples, dedication, and commitment to strengthening families. Thanks also to Barbara and Hal Jones for their friendship. Appreciation goes to our families—especially our wives, Debi Wilcox and Aimee Robbins. And finally, we wouldn't be in the position we are today if it weren't for our own parents' persistence and selflessness when we were young. Thank you to Ray and Val Wilcox and Rob and Liz Robbins for connecting with us when we were teenagers. We love them and are so grateful for their support of us and our dreams.

Contents

Introduction

How to Hug a Hedgehog

" I don't want to hug that one!" said three-year-old Paisley as she pointed to an alligator. Brad was taking his granddaughters to the zoo, and Paisley, the eldest, was dividing the entire animal kingdom into two groups: huggable and not huggable. The koalas were huggable; the alligators were not.

Brad encouraged the game as they went from enclosure to enclosure by asking, "Would you hug this one?" He was a little surprised when Paisley said yes to the giraffes and flamingos. He was not surprised when snakes got a no. Paisley decided that lions were huggable (blame that one on animated movies), but declared that porcupines and hedgehogs were definitely not huggable. Most would agree on that one. In fact, that is why zoos have barriers and cages—to keep us from close contact with such animals.

Outside of zoos, it's a different story. We all know teenagers who look and act as prickly as hedgehogs and have successfully erected barriers around themselves to keep us out. While we are better off leaving the "un-huggable" zoo animals alone, we actually want and need to have a connection with bristly teenagers—for their sakes and ours. In a zoo, we shouldn't try to bypass cages and ignore the "Keep Out" signs. In our families, we have to have the determination and personal courage to brave all barriers and connect with even the most difficult teenagers. Wild animals are best left wild. Deep down, teenagers long for connections. They need and appreciate loving and positive relationships with parents and other adults who care enough to reach out to them, despite the quills.

Hedgehogs are nocturnal. They become active at dusk and spend most of the day sleeping. Does that sound like some teenagers you know? Hedgehogs eat mostly insects. They don't have a very balanced diet. Hmm. Hedgehogs don't like being caged. They would rather be outside roaming and exploring. That all sounds familiar as well. Hedgehogs (and some teenagers) can be stubborn creatures, resisting change at every turn. Unlike many teenagers, hedgehogs are clean and have very little smell. Of course, the most prominent feature of the hedgehog is his sharp quills—hollow hairs that can be dangerous when extended. Teenagers have similar defenses.

Anyone who works in a zoo knows there are some principles that can make all the difference when working with dangerous animals. Those who work with children and teenagers know there are some principles that also make a difference. There are painful ways to hug a hedgehog and smart ways. Believe it or not, hedgehogs can make great pets.

Rules for Hugging a Hedgehog:

1. Don't wear gloves; let him sniff you.
2. Take your time; let him relax. If he rolls into a ball and extends his quills, stay calm and be patient.
3. With both hands, scoop him up from the belly, which is covered in soft fur rather than quills. Let him explore you and become more comfortable with you.

No two hedgehogs are alike, but these general rules apply to most. No two teenagers are alike either, but there are some keys parents can learn that will help. The following pages are filled with a variety of suggestions that have worked for us. They center on establishing and maintaining communication, overcoming adversity, and building self-esteem. At the end of each chapter, you will find invitations to action that, if accepted, can help you put into practice the principles being presented. Our hope is that this book can validate the positive efforts you are already making and provide a friendly nudge in new directions if necessary.

When Brad was at the zoo with his granddaughters, Paisley's invented game was fun, but it didn't last. Our efforts to connect with teens must be conscious and consistent. Our success or failure will have lifelong consequences for all involved. We must find ways to bypass the barriers and reach out to even the most prickly teen. Hugging a hedgehog may be a unique challenge, but it is not vital. Building positive relationships with teenagers is absolutely essential and will enrich and transform all of our lives forever.

Improve
Communication

How to Hug a Hedgehog: Rule #1

"Don't wear gloves; let him sniff you."

As a hedgehog gets to know you through sniffing, he becomes more comfortable with you and easier for you to hug. As teenagers and parents get to know each other through effective verbal and nonverbal communication, we all become more comfortable. Parents can improve communication with teenagers through four keys: sensing teens' unspoken needs, bringing down the walls between parents and teenagers, spending time together, and setting and maintaining appropriate limits.

Chapter 1

Hear Them Cry

"It's as though there's a wall there," one mother said. "When my daughter was younger, it was easy to communicate with her. We talked regularly and openly. But as she got older, this wall went up." She shook her head. "Why won't she talk to me anymore?"

This mother is not alone in her frustration. Many parents know about the walls teenagers sometimes build. These walls seem high and impenetrable. Some even appear to be covered with barbed wire and jolted with high-voltage electricity. Yet, walls can come down, as evidenced by the famous dismantling of a wall in Berlin, Germany.

The Berlin Wall was nearly fourteen feet high, covered with barbed wire, and plastered with "Stay Away" signs. It was built to keep people isolated. But it couldn't last forever, and in 1989, the wall that had separated families and friends for so long was torn down. On Brad's desk is a little chunk of that wall—a small piece of concrete with an inch-long piece of barbed wire. The concrete has some faded colors on one side. It may seem like a strange choice for a desktop decoration, but it serves as a reminder that even the highest and most formidable walls built to keep people separated can come down.

Sometimes teenagers build invisible walls around themselves. They may build them for protection, or perhaps because of feelings of insecurity, distrust, fear, or misunderstanding. How can parents most effectively penetrate such barriers? How do we talk to teens who don't particularly want to talk to us? How do we make ourselves into the kind of people our children will open up to? We must first see beyond the wall and then find the loose brick.

See Beyond the Wall

Some teenagers wear extreme hairstyles, torn jeans, long chains, and baggy t-shirts. Some have tattoos and use vulgar words and gestures. Others are well-groomed but act cocky, rude, and defiant. Still others seem distant and unmotivated. In all of these cases, adults receive strong signals that seem to say, "Leave me alone and stay out of my life." We must see beyond the façade.

Teenagers' emotions and needs are usually expressed in coded messages—secret codes, if you will—that we must receive and interpret. It's really nothing new. Remember when your children were babies? They cried, and you didn't know why. You tried changing them; still they cried. You tried feeding them, rocking them. You thought, "I can't figure these kids out! I wish they could just talk to me and tell me what they want!"

Now those little ones are teenagers, and they are still playing the same game. They no longer need a diaper change or bottle. They need security, acceptance, attention, and positive feedback. But they don't voice those needs any more clearly now than when they were babies. They just give you the signals and expect you to figure out what they need. In their own way, your teens are still crying. Only now, the tears are inside.

Kenneth Cope once wrote a song about those silent tears. The first lines say, "There's a cry in the night as another life begins. Tiny one pleads for love today." Kenneth's lyrics then describe how children grow and their cries turn inward. Our favorite line in the song is a question: "Can wounds concealed be recognized?" It is up to us to "hear them cry the tears they hide. Love means time. Hear them cry."[1]

Do you love me? Do you care? Am I a priority in your life? Such questions rarely come directly from teenagers, but they do come indirectly. Often, the most important part of communication is being able to hear what isn't being said. Just as all parents struggle to interpret the cries of babies, we have to do a lot of guessing, testing, and putting ourselves in teenagers' shoes to begin to understand their unspoken messages. What are they feeling from behind their walls? Are they feeling insecure, ugly, untalented, stupid, scared, lonely, rejected, frustrated, or vulnerable? Here are some of the clues that help us look beyond the walls and hear teenagers crying.

Creating distance. If teenagers pull away from the family and appear to be vague, withdrawn, or evasive, it is often a silent cry. When they don't look us in the eyes when we are talking or they avoid us when we are coming in their direction, we know there are tears falling inside. Of course, the natural reaction is to also pull back and tell ourselves, "I know when I'm not wanted," or "If that's how she feels about me, then I won't push myself into her life," or "If he's not going to talk to me, then I won't talk to him." We must fight this natural tendency. We need to act rather than react to our teenagers.

One father, who has reared ten sons and three daughters, described how he searched for answers when one of his teenage sons became distant: "The greatest revelation I got from all the reading I did was this simple but profound thought: whether my son spoke to me or not didn't change the fact that I could speak to him. Even if it was just one-way communication, at least he'd know how I felt. And I felt that this would keep the channels open so that he would always know that I would be there if he needed me." This father approached his son and said, "I know a little bit about what you're going through. I just want you to know that I know you can do it, that I love you and have confidence in you." The boy didn't respond, but he heard. The father didn't follow his natural tendency to pull away from his son; instead, he kept communication open and was able to show his son that he cared about him. The father acted.

Adolescents, however, find it difficult to know how to act. Are they supposed to be big children or little adults? Moping around and pulling away are ways some teenagers mentally try on new roles to see how they fit. When this happens, hear them cry.

Extreme behavior. Teenagers who tend to be either extremely quiet or extremely loud are trying to communicate something from behind the wall. "That kid is so cocky. He needs a good humbling," or "She's really shy, don't bother talking to her," we might say when, in reality, both teens need just the opposite—to be built up and validated. Pretended pride or shyness is nothing more than a strategy teens use because inside they are feeling small, passed over, unimportant, or envious of others.

Teenagers who are extremely judgmental and can't find one good thing to say about any other person are probably trying desperately to find one good thing they like about themselves. Hear them cry.

"I have a friend who . . ." Jerrick remembers a time when he came home from school and told his parents, "I have a friend who really wants to go watch a movie that might have some bad things in it, but he says it'll be OK if he just closes his eyes. What would you say to him?"

Rather than saying something like, "I'd probably tell you to go find another friend," or making quick judgments about this "friend," Jerrick's parents listened to him explain the entire situation. True, Jerrick's friend was thinking about going to that movie, but so was he. He knew that he shouldn't view what might be on the movie screen because it violated family rules, but he thought it might be OK if he just closed his eyes. Instead of directly asking his parents if that was OK, Jerrick asked about his friend to discover how his parents would respond.

Whenever a child tells you about "my friend's" problem, there is a good chance that child is struggling with a similar one. Young people drop hints about "friends" to test our reactions. If we are hasty and harsh, they may not want to open up any further. Hold off on judgments long enough to hear them cry.

Nonverbal signals. Very little of what a person says is with words. Most of our communication comes through body language. Our tone of voice also sends untold messages to the listener. Thus, it is important for parents to learn to listen with their eyes and hearts as well as with their ears. In short, we must be aware that teenagers' true attitudes and feelings are usually expressed through gestures, posture, rate of speech, voice tone, volume, and eye placement.

We need to notice the expression on their faces, the look in their eyes, and the way they hold their heads. We can detect boredom, hostility, or fatigue by simply observing the fidgeting of their legs and the movement of their hands. Watch carefully for nonverbal signals. Hear them cry.

Seeking attention. With children, overtly negative behavior is often just a ploy to attract attention. The same thing is true of teenagers. Childish pranks like giggling at inappropriate times and pulling hair give way to swearing, extreme styles of clothing, body piercings, offensive hand motions, outlandish hairstyles, and tattoos. All such overt behavior is sending the same message: "Pay attention to me. Please notice me as an individual and appreciate the fact that I am different."

When teenagers make rash statements such as "I hate school" or "My teacher is an idiot," they often just want someone to notice they are frustrated. We must be careful not to take at face value the "wrong" things young people do or say. In such situations, young people may not feel unsure about what is "right" so much as they feel unsure about themselves. Hear them cry.

Inconsistent behavior. Any difference between usual behavior and current behavior is often a cry for help. One girl who consistently did well in school suddenly started missing the bus. When her mom would ask her if she was ready to go, the girl would say, "I'm coming." Then she'd wait around until she missed the bus and her mother had to take her to school.

The mother tried to reason with her daughter, telling her, "This is ridiculous. You're a mature, responsible person. You shouldn't need to be babied along in the morning." The girl agreed and caught the bus the next few days. Then she began missing it again. The mother said, "This is not like you. I have always been able to count on you. If you miss the bus again, I'll take you, but you'll have to pay me."

The following morning, the mother ended up having to drive the girl to school. When they arrived, she said, "That will be three dollars and a thank-you."

The girl blew up. "Taxi drivers don't get thanked!" she said indignantly.

The mother drove away from the school with her daughter still in the car. At last, she had heard her daughter's cries. The mother said, "We need to talk." The girl finally admitted she was having a hard time in her first-period class. She did not understand the teacher and was feeling stupid. There were also some boys in that class who were teasing her. Now mother and daughter were finally addressing the real problems, which had very little to do with catching a school bus. When teenagers' behavior is inconsistent, hear them cry. After hearing them cry, we must then find the "loose brick" in the walls they've built around themselves.

Find the "Loose Brick"

"The thing about my mom that I love is that she likes what I like, even though she's old," a teenager explained. "She doesn't think that what I like is stupid or just some passing fad. She doesn't say my tastes are immature."

Brad's friend who had worked in construction once taught him a valuable principle about breaking down walls when he stated, "Having laid a few brick walls in my time, I have discovered that every wall has a weakness, a brick that is loose."

When we work with young people who have built walls around themselves, we must find the loose brick—the one favorite interest, dream, or ability that will help that teen open up. It may be motorcycles, sports, food, the opposite sex, or even a journal.

One young man from New York who attended a week-long youth program on the west coast stayed to himself at first. His youth counselor was concerned and told the program director,

"He just stays in his room and writes in his journal." Was this the loose brick the director needed?

That evening at dinner, the director purposely sat by the young man in the cafeteria. He began a normal conversation and then changed the subject to journals. The director said, "People don't usually believe me when I say it, but one of my favorite things to do is to write in my journal. I've already filled many volumes."

"Really?" The boy's eyes lit up. "I write in my journal, too. I think it's important." That was a turning point. The young man began to come to activities and to interact with the director and others. Before the week ended, he had made many new friends. It all started when someone showed a little interest in his big interest.

During Jerrick's freshman year of high school, he developed a serious stomach illness that baffled his doctors. They weren't sure why he was feeling so sick, but they were determined to find the cause. Jerrick was put through many different tests to rule out certain diseases.

The day before one of those tests—a colonoscopy—Jerrick was feeling particularly nervous. Considering a test like that, who wouldn't be? After an entire day of eating nothing but plain yellow Jell-O, chicken broth, and yummy magnesium citrate, his nerves were completely on edge. Normally, he'd play sports or eat ice cream to calm himself, but those options weren't available, so he went downstairs and started to play billiards—a game he loved— by himself.

A few minutes later, his dad came downstairs and started to play with him. After a couple questions, Jerrick opened up to his dad about what he was feeling at the time. Jerrick would never have spoken with his dad about his fears if his dad had not been willing to come downstairs and play billiards.

A teacher once attended a farewell party for a former student who was going off to college. The young man looked ready for college. He had new clothes and his hair had been cut just the day before. He was smiling confidently. His parents knew that the boy's lifestyle hadn't always been as neat as his hair was now. He was never a bad kid. He hadn't done anything terribly wrong. But the boy had withdrawn from everyone and had certainly ruled out ever attending college. It seemed as if no one could reach him. Then the teacher had come into his life and finally gotten through the wall.

Later, the parents asked the teacher how he had successfully reached this young man who had managed to distance himself so completely from everyone else. Had the teacher shared a special story or personal experience? Had he carried on long and in-depth talks with the boy? The teacher only smiled and said, "You'll never believe it, but one day I found out your boy likes reruns of the same old TV show I like. Your son would come up to me after class to discuss the show. He would bring me information about how much some of the old props and costumes were being auctioned for and where all those old actors are now." The teacher had stumbled upon the loose brick. Then he worked at it until he opened a space in the wall of isolation around the young man.

After Brad talked at a parent conference about finding the loose brick, a mother approached Brad and said, "But there is no way to reach my daughter. She simply does not have any loose bricks—a few loose screws, maybe, but no loose bricks."

"Sure she does," Brad assured her. "What does she talk about or bring up in conversation?"

"Nothing."

"What does she do in her free time if she can choose?"

"Nothing. She just goes to school and works."

"Then what does she do with the money she earns?"

"She buys lots of clothes," the mother answered, rolling her eyes.

Brad smiled at her and said, "Guess what you just found."

Three questions: What does your teenager talk most about? What does your teenager do or want to do with free time? Where does your teenager put his or her own money? Answers to these can help us locate that loose brick. Then it is just a matter of spending the time required to push and pull at it until we break through.

A woman learned how important it is to see beyond the wall and find the loose brick when her daughter was fifteen years old. That summer, her daughter attended a state-run camp in California, a camp she had looked forward to all year. But after she came home, this mother noticed a big change in her daughter. She was more distant from the family. Her moods were extreme. She wasn't taking care of her appearance, which was inconsistent for her.

At the time, the woman did not recognize the cries she was hearing. She didn't think of approaching her daughter to talk. Problems continued, and finally she knew that she needed to do something about it.

One evening, her daughter went babysitting and left her journal open by the front door. That was not like her at all. The woman picked it up and began to read. The more she read, the more horrified she became. A camp mentor with whom her daughter had been corresponding was participating in some illegal activities and inviting the girl to join her. This woman said, "I cannot tell you what I felt at that time. I took the journal and showed my husband. He was irate that this mentor had been allowed to work with young girls at the camp. He wanted the people responsible to realize what was happening."

In the meantime, the woman didn't know what to do about her daughter. She talked with her dearest friends. They all advised her to seek professional help. She went to three different psychologists until she found the one who gave her the advice that really made sense to her.

The counselor told the woman that she had to talk with her daughter openly about the whole thing. Nothing could have been more frightening for her. It seemed much easier to just keep going through her mothering motions as if nothing were wrong. The counselor told her that she had to be honest with her daughter and even tell her she had read her journal.

The next day, the woman sat down with her daughter and told her everything. Her daughter was absolutely devastated that her mother had violated her privacy.

This concerned mother simply said, "The friend you are writing to is on the wrong track. She is much older than you, and I feel very strongly that staying friends with her is dangerous for you."

Her daughter ran out of the room in tears. Easy experience? No. Fun? No. Necessary? Yes. Did the woman handle it the way she should? She didn't know. She was simply doing the best she knew how.

In the days that followed, the counselor advised her to spend more time bonding with her daughter. She had raised her daughter the same way she had raised her son, and now she realized that certain children need more love and attention. She thought that perhaps because she didn't give her daughter all the love she needed, her daughter was searching elsewhere for a sense of belonging. The counselor told her not to blame herself, but instead to try to communicate, to let her daughter talk, and then to listen to her.

The woman didn't know where to begin. She did not think about loose bricks at the time. She felt overwhelmed by the task ahead of her. "My teenage daughter hated me so much," she said. "I can still feel the horrible feeling in the pit of my stomach when I think about it. It is such a hopeless feeling when your own child hates you."

She knew her daughter didn't care to be with her right then, but she also knew that her daughter was fifteen and cared a lot about being in a car. She told her, "OK, you want to learn to drive a car, right? I'll pick you up after school every day so you can practice."

Each afternoon, this mother would pick up her daughter, who would climb into the car, slam the door, and not say a word. The mom would let her practice driving a while, and then she would say, "I haven't eaten anything since breakfast. Would you mind if we stop at the bakery for a bagel?"

Day after day, they would sit in the bakery, eating their bagels in silence. Eventually, her daughter started talking. She would tell her mother about her day. Then she started telling her mother about the things that were going on in her life. It took almost the entire year, but things did start to get better. This woman had to give up some control in exchange for some trust, but it was worth it.

Many years later, the woman's daughter went on to graduate from high school and was preparing to go out of state for college. The two of them sat on the floor of the bedroom and packed. The daughter came across her old journals. She opened one and read to her mother all the things she had been going through during that dark time in her life. She confessed that she had even considered committing suicide. She looked at her mother and said, "Mom, I'm so glad I didn't do that. I'm so glad we became friends."

When trying to connect with teenagers, you'll notice they can put up walls that seem as impenetrable as the hedgehog's quills. Rather than wearing gloves, you need to connect with and address the hedgehog directly; and rather than avoiding confrontation, we need to hear the cries of your teenagers early. Find the loose brick—the one thing teenagers want to do or to talk about enough that they will even put up with having you there. Then listen carefully, communicate openly, and be there for them. You'll be surprised what they will say to you, what they can teach you, and how well they'll respond to even your most awkward efforts.

Invitations to Action

How can you hear and respond to your teenager's silent cries? How can you get through to him or her? Here are some questions to consider:

- Looking back on your own life, what type of walls have you put up? How could people have seen beyond those walls?

- What are some of your teenager's hobbies or favorite things? How can you show more interest in those hobbies? How can you also learn to value those favorite things?

Endnotes:

1. Kenneth, Cope. "Hear Them Cry," from *Voices* (Lightware Records, 1991).

Chapter 2

Dismantle the Wall

Jerrick remembers a time when he was tasked with demolishing a retaining wall in a backyard. He went up to the wall, armed with a sledgehammer, thinking that the job would be easy job and would take a couple hours at most. What he didn't realize until examining the wall more closely was that this particular wall, rather than having mortar laid on top of each layer of bricks to provide support for further layers, had concrete poured straight down the center of each brick with pieces of steel rebar inserted to provide even better stability. *This seems impossible*, Jerrick thought.

As the day progressed and the sun beat down on his red, sunburned neck, Jerrick kept swinging away at that wall. Eventually, he was able to knock one brick loose from the others. Once that loose brick was removed, the stability of the entire wall was compromised, and it was a lot easier to knock the rest of it down.

When working with teenagers who have built a wall around themselves, we must first see beyond the wall and then find that loose brick—the one interest, dream, hobby, or ability that will let us penetrate their concrete-enforced, rebar-studded wall. Once the loose brick is discovered, we can work on completely dismantling the walls in order to connect with teenagers and help them in their quest for adulthood.

Effective communication is the tool that will help to completely dismantle the walls children build around themselves. It might take a lot of swings to start, but the wall will come down eventually. Three essential elements of open communication are love, trust, and respect.

Love

A teenager once told us, "I wish my dad would hug me more and show affection to me when something's wrong or if I'm having a bad day. He used to do so when I was growing up, and it was a good feeling. It's not that I doubt my father's love, it's just that sometimes I need him to tell me he cares for me no matter what I'm doing. I don't feel a lot of love inside of me right now."

Perhaps the reason some parents have difficulty talking with teenagers is the way we, as parents, communicate our love. Usually, we tend to take on more of an authoritative role. We dictate rules, demand accountability, and then, if teens comply and put together a good enough track record, finally convey our approval and love. This is backwards.

Our caring and love must be constant and unconditional—given first and given freely through good or bad, right or wrong, brilliant success or utter failure. Regardless of their choices, teenagers need our nonjudgmental love. It becomes the only secure base upon which expectations and accountability can then be built.

One young man finally gathered the courage to discuss some of his past mistakes with a trusted uncle. At the end of the conversation, the young man said, "I feel embarrassed about unloading all this on you. What do you think of me?"

Without a pause, the uncle said, "I love you for it. There isn't anything you could share with me that would cause me to love you less." The young man and his uncle enjoyed not only continued open communication but also a deeper friendship from that time forward.

Brad attended a youth gathering in Arkansas where young people came from many different areas, and no one seemed to know anyone else. Everyone was feeling a little insecure and uncomfortable.

At the back of the room, he noticed a boy with fully grown hands on the ends of stubs at his shoulders, but no arms. Everyone walked past without looking at him. You could almost sense that each one was thinking, *My mom told me not to stare at people who are different.* That day, Brad learned that the opposite of love is not hate. Rather, it is indifference. Even hate recognizes that someone is standing there.

He wondered, *How am I going to involve this boy?* On the other side of the room, he saw another boy who stood alone. He was heavyset and obviously feeling out of place. Brad thought to himself, *This is perfect.* He introduced the two boys to each other and said firmly, "Now, you two be friends."

They didn't argue. They just said, "OK." Those boys stayed together during all the activities. By the end, they really had become good friends.

At the final dance, Brad was dancing in the middle of the dance floor when he suddenly felt that someone was staring at him. He turned, and there behind him stood the boy with no arms. Music was blaring and teenagers were dancing all around them, but the boy didn't move.

Finally he said, "Mr. Wilcox, my friend and I want to invite you to our pizza party after the dance."

Brad smiled and said, "I'm honored. I'd be happy to come. You can count on it."

The boy looked at his buddy at the side of the room, gave him a thumbs-up signal, and then turned back to Brad and added, "Mr. Wilcox, we need a phone to call and order the pizza."

Brad smiled and told him where his briefcase was, adding, "Find my cell phone and go order us some pizza." The two buddies left excitedly, and Brad turned back to his dancing.

About half an hour later, he felt eyes staring at him again. Sure enough, it was that same boy. "Mr. Wilcox," he said, "we called and ordered the pizza like you said, but"—he hesitated—"now we need thirteen dollars to pay for it."

Some pizza party! Brad thought. *They invite me to their pizza party, and I am buying.* He chuckled and told the boy, "You know where my briefcase is. Go ahead and find my wallet. Pull out thirteen dollars."

Brad expected another thumbs-up signal. Instead, the young man just stood there looking at him. His eyes filled with tears. All he said was, "Really? You'd do that for me?"

Brad grabbed him and hugged him. Then he looked directly into this new friend's eyes and said, "Listen, you are worth so much more to me than thirteen dollars."

Unconditional love and caring can mean everything to young people. (Incidentally, Brad once shared the above story at another youth conference. Afterward, some of the group came up and said, "Mr. Wilcox, we want to invite you to our steak and lobster party!")

Love is felt often but expressed rarely. Love must be made visible by actions and words. One young woman wrote a letter in which she talked about fighting with her mother and finally making up. "I wondered what I could say to make up with my mom," she wrote, "but I didn't have to think long because on Sunday my mom hugged me and said, 'I love you,' and I guess our hearts could just feel each other's pain. Right then we knew we had forgiven each other."

Touch is one of the most important ways we have to express love. Unlike many adults, most children welcome and even seek touch. Experts claim it is an actual need for children, one that is as essential as their need for food and water. But as adults, we try to convince ourselves otherwise, saying, "That's just not me anymore. Touchy-feely is not my style." Yet experts say that, even for adults, touching is a primary means of communicating, whether we're conscious of it or not. We never outgrow our need for feeling—literally feeling—love.

Jerrick remembers a time when he was preparing to leave home and move to another state. His parents were excited for him, but they were a bit nervous, like any parents would be when a child moves away from home. Just before he left, Jerrick and his mom were talking about some of the fears Jerrick was having about leaving home. After their talk, Jerrick's mom reached over and gave his hand a good squeeze. No words were communicated between the two of them, but Jerrick felt and understood through that tender touch that his mom understood him, cared about him, and loved him very much.

Brad once had the opportunity to visit with inmates at a maximum-security prison. He spoke with one man who was led into the room with his ankles chained together and his hands chained at his wrists. Because Brad knew this man's background and his family, he greeted him with a big *abrazo* or "hug." The man began to cry. Softly, he said, "That is the first hug I have received in over three years!"

Brad's friends always tease him that his motto must be, "If it moves, hug it!" We are well aware of the cautions and guidelines given for personal and professional interactions. We understand the concern for appropriateness. Still, many young people, large and small, have clung to Brad and hugged him until he could hardly breathe. He has seen teenagers wait in lines because they were hungering for the acknowledgment and acceptance that come with a simple hug. He has held teenagers like little children and rocked them back and forth in his arms as they have sobbed on his shoulders. Jerrick has experienced times when no words needed to be said because of the feelings expressed through a simple hug to a discouraged family member or struggling friend. He has seen firsthand how a hug can communicate gratitude to a helpful relative, love to a saddened adult, and comfort to an injured child. There is a need to respect personal space, but sometimes there are more important needs that must also be met.

After receiving a much-needed hug from Brad, one young man wrote: "Except for once with my father, I had never hugged a man before—not even my brothers. Thank you. That hug filled me with a glow that lasted through several days." A girl wrote, "I had never had a hug from anyone in my entire life. I've wanted one. Oh, how I've longed for one, but I'm sorry because when I hugged you I didn't even know where to put my arms or anything. I'd never done that before—ever."

These young people were starved for something that has absolutely nothing to do with passion or sex. They were starved for the validation and affirmation that come through touch. Remember, you aren't making any sexual statements by giving a hug. You're making a statement about human love and caring. In Scandinavia, the Norse word *hugga* means "to comfort, hold close, or console." As we hug someone, including (and maybe especially) our teenagers, we can give them something they desperately need—comfort and a sense of belonging.

Another essential expression of love involves actually saying the words "I love you." One girl wrote, "I believe my mom doesn't love me because I have never heard 'I love you' come out of her mouth for sixteen years. I say, 'I love you, Mom' and she says, 'I know.' Is that normal?"

Jerrick comes from a large family, but while he and his siblings were growing up, his parents made sure they told each child that they loved him or her individually. In addition, they knew that each child responded to affection in different ways. Jerrick's sisters loved it when their parents spent time reading them bedtime stories, so they would. Jerrick, on the other hand, would rather read his own stories. He liked it when his parents supported him by attending his sporting events, like volleyball and basketball games. To show their love, Jerrick's parents took time to come support him at his games and tournaments.

Reading stories and attending sporting events was how Jerrick's parents communicated their love to each child individually, but they also provided times when they could say the words "I love you." Jerrick's parents made sure they told their children they loved them and gave them hugs and kisses goodnight—even if Jerrick and some of his brothers thought they were too cool for that. Looking back, Jerrick treasures those memories because the words "I love you" gave additional power to his parents' actions of love.

Mother Teresa, a woman respected around the world for her work with the poor of Calcutta, received the Nobel Peace Prize in 1979. During her acceptance lecture, she said, "I want you to find the poor here, right in your own home first. And begin love there."[i] We can't think of a better place to start.

"I love you. I'm proud of you. I've missed you. I'm lucky to have you." Such words are more important than we realize and will bring us that much closer to open communication with our teenagers.

Trust

Trust is also important in communication. One parent asked, "How can I trust my teen? He is totally untrustworthy." The truth of the matter is, we don't have a choice. We can't follow children around the rest of their lives. Even as adults, are we always trustworthy? Perhaps we should focus on our children's potential and not on their current problems. Our children need messages of trust from us. We must find ways to allow them enough freedom to grow and enough boundaries to provide safety and security.

Trusting relationships can be established by keeping confidences. During the weekends while Jerrick was still in high school, he and his parents would stay up late and discuss pretty much anything from sports to politics. Often, those conversations would turn personal as Jerrick shared with his parents his struggles with low self-esteem, classes at school, and peer pressure. Never did his parents share those personal conversations with others—including Jerrick's own siblings. Because of the confidence Jerrick had in his parents' ability to keep his secrets, he trusted them more and confided in them continually.

Another way to gain trust is to compliment young people. Too often, by being overly critical or sarcastic with comments like "This kitchen still looks dirty," "Are you ever going to do better than a B?" or "That'll be the day," parents take the clumsy position of blocking the very communication doors we want our children to enter. Children may put up with put-downs, but no one appreciates insults. They may laugh and play along, but deep down, it hurts. Children remember and replay hurtful comments to themselves for years. On the other hand, positive compliments can create open lines of communication.

Jerrick remembers an English teacher he had in high school—Mr. Parker—who was excellent at giving positive compliments. Every paper that Jerrick wrote in that class was meticulously looked over, but along with critiques, there were plenty of compliments. Although comments on the paper might say something like "Consider revising your word order," or "Watch your subject-verb agreement," they also lavished praise: "I love the alliteration here," "Great word choice," and "Excellent transition sentence." Because of those sincere compliments, Jerrick felt like he could trust his teacher and often went to him for advice about writing and about life.

Young people appreciate it when we notice nice things about them and mention them with sincerity. Superlatives like "greatest," "smartest," and "best" may run a little ahead of reality, but remember, compliments expressed are often the seedbed of dreams fulfilled. Let us speak the language of possibility and hope.

We destroy trust when we are rude or cynical. Despite what the writers of comedy shows would have us believe, cutting remarks are not humorous or witty so much as they are hurtful and mean. When we criticize any person, we not only alienate that one person but also send a signal to other people that someday they will be next. Kind words offer safety and security in a teenager's fearful world.

As a teenager, Brad was self-conscious about how he came across when speaking to groups. On one particular occasion, he was called on with no prior warning to speak in front of a large group. After it was over, he was sure he had made a total idiot of himself. Then a note was passed down the aisle where he was sitting. He thought it was going to be from some of the other teenagers saying how stupid he sounded. Instead, it was from Mr. Allen, one of his teachers. The note said, "Good job. I'm sure proud of you." Mr. Allen's words couldn't have been more needed. They lifted Brad up more than Mr. Allen will ever know. Brad kept that note in his wallet until it became dog-eared.

One junior high school teacher learned through many years of experience the value of giving his students compliments. Each year, he noticed students in his classes who came from very difficult family situations—some were homeless, orphaned, or from abusive backgrounds. This teacher always complimented his students when they did well, but he put forth extra effort to praise those students who needed extra support. He noticed that often those students would start out class either very shy or very disruptive. Although he still gave appropriate consequences for bad behavior, the compliments he gave those students eventually created a feeling of trust between the students and teacher.

He remembers one time when a student of his who was normally very attentive fell asleep during class. The teacher didn't embarrass her or call attention to it. After class, he approached the student one-on-one and asked her why she was so tired.

She said, "My dad didn't get home until late last night, so I had to take care of my siblings." The rest of their conversation revealed that the girl's mom had left the family during the summer, and this teacher was able to help direct the child toward some counseling services that she desperately needed.

"If I hadn't created that relationship of trust with my student earlier with some simple compliments," he said, "I seriously doubt that she would have opened up to me like that. If I had teased or humiliated her for falling asleep, she would never have shared her problems with such honesty."

Respect

Showing respect for young people allows for open communication. In one instance, a woman and her husband were approached by a community leader and asked if, since they had a spacious home, they would mind hosting a lunch for the guest speaker, a famous author, coming to a large conference. They gladly agreed.

This woman explained how she and her husband planned the menu, cleaned the entire house, and set out their best china. After all, this famous author was coming to visit their home, and they wanted to show proper respect.

On the morning of the anticipated conference, they were putting the final touches on everything. Their teenage son came downstairs for breakfast. He ate some cereal and then, knowing it was a special day, cleaned up after himself. He even rinsed the bowl—but left it in the sink.

This woman said, "When I went to the kitchen and saw that bowl in the sink, I exploded. I yelled at my son and gave him a talking-to he would not soon forget." The bowl was hidden. The family left to attend the conference.

Through the whole meeting, the mother kept looking over at her son sitting there several seats away. She knew she had overreacted, and she felt guilty. She said, "I realized that while trying so hard to show respect to the speaker who would visit my home later that day, I had failed to show respect for the boy who lives there every day. Didn't my son deserve the same respect I was extending to this other person?"

She reached across her younger children, tapped her son on his shoulder, and mouthed the words, "I'm sorry. Will you forgive me?"

The quality of our communication with our children will improve in direct proportion to the amount of respect we show them when we talk together. One of the most obvious ways to show respect is by listening. In fact, we should usually do quite a bit more listening than talking.

Effective listening requires time, intent, and a temporary suspending of judgments and advice. When teenagers are upset or discouraged, they don't need solutions to problems so much as they need understanding sounding boards. Right answers are usually obvious.

Maybe you're thinking, *So am I supposed to just sit there with my mouth shut?* The answer is yes. Silence can be a potent sign of acceptance and respect. Face the teenager, keep eye contact, and nod occasionally to show interest. But stay quiet and you'll be amazed at the quality and quantity of comments you are able to draw out.

Sometimes another effective listening response is to paraphrase in our own words the messages we hear. This shows we comprehend what the teenager means. We can also say such things as "I see" and "I understand"—comments that show we are relating to what the teenager feels.

If a famous speaker and author came to our home, would we watch TV or fold clothes while he or she was trying to speak to us? Would we interrupt or correct his or her grammar? Showing proper respect for teenagers will improve our communication and relationship with them.

Eventually, teenage walls will come tumbling down. One teacher came to school to find his students had decorated his office. For him, it was better than a raise. One father found a card from his son left on his pillow, a gift that, for him, was priceless. Days after Jerrick taught a class as a substitute teacher, one of the students recognized him and approached him to let him know how much he appreciated his teaching style. Who thanks a substitute teacher? Jerrick was thrilled. Every parent can have similar experiences.

Since hedgehogs are nocturnal, they rely on smell rather than sight to distinguish friend from foe. Wearing gloves blocks your distinct smell, but taking the gloves off allows the hedgehog to recognize you. Likewise, when we, as parents, "take the gloves off" and show teenagers—truly and genuinely—that we love them, trust them, and respect them, teenagers will recognize and respond to that openness and sincerity. Those three keys, "I love you," "I trust you," and "I respect you," will allow for effective communication with teenagers if we use them often. The walls will come tumbling down. If we want love, trust, and respect from teenagers, we must give these things to teenagers first, and then give them again and again. It may not happen right away, but with constant effort, we can gain the love, trust, and respect of our teenagers.

Invitations to Action

How can you dismantle teenage walls that hinder us in connecting with them? Here are keys that will help:

- How does your teenager respond to the way you show love to him or her? Are there other ways you could demonstrate your love?

- Think of people you trust. How did you get to that point with them? How can you create more trust in your relationship with your teenager?

- How do you show your teenager that you respect him or her? How can you engage in listening to your teenager?

Endnotes:

1. Mother Teresa, "Nobel Lecture," 11 December 1979, from nobelprize.org.

Chapter 3

Enjoy Dinner Conversations

What was the best dinner you've ever had? Was it at a wedding, a company luncheon, or a family function? Was it in a fancy restaurant high up in a skyscraper overlooking your favorite city? Was it in an old, family-run establishment with sawdust on the floor and service that can't be beat? Or was it at home, with a perfectly cooked Thanksgiving turkey in the center of a table surrounded by family?

Whatever your favorite dinner was, it wasn't just the food that made the dinner memorable. It might have been the setting, it might have been the mood, or it might have been the service. More likely, though, it was the company. We may forget the main course of a dinner, but we'll always remember the magnificent conversations we have while we eat. One of the best ways to connect with teenagers is spending time together, and meal time is a great place to start.

Anyone who has ever dealt with teenagers knows that teenagers love to eat! We know a couple with five sons. When those boys became teenagers, the couple had to buy an extra refrigerator just to keep up with demand. However, teenagers don't need good food as much as they need good company. Teenagers need a big helping of family conversation with their food.

A 2007 study done by the National Center on Addiction and Substance Abuse at Columbia University discovered significant ties to family dinners:

> Compared to teens who eat dinner frequently with their families (five or more family dinners per week), those who have infrequent family dinners (fewer than three per week) are:
>
> ○ three and a half times likelier to have abused prescription drugs
>
> ○ three and a half times likelier to have used an illegal drug other than marijuana or prescription drugs
>
> ○ three times likelier to have used marijuana
>
> ○ more than two and a half times likelier to have used tobacco
>
> ○ one and a half times likelier to have used alcohol[1]

Those may be some harrowing statistics, but the study also found that among teenagers who earn mostly A's and B's at school, 64 percent report that they have family dinner 5–7 times per week. Striving to have family dinner together is clearly worth it, but it can be difficult in today's busy world.

Parents often assume that because teenagers sometimes whine and complain about having to eat dinner with the family, they must not want to eat with the family. That's a common misconception. When asked if they wanted to have dinner with family, "84 percent of teens surveyed say they prefer to have dinner with their families, compared to 13 percent who say they prefer to eat dinner alone."[2] Even though teenagers' actions might suggest otherwise, we must see beyond the acting and recognize that teenagers need and desire dinner conversations. We can then try our hardest to make dinnertime become family time. As families come together around the dinner table, they will connect because of the conversations they will share together. We have compiled some suggestions to help parents make the most of that time with their teenagers. As parents make family dinnertime a priority, divide dinner responsibilities, limit technology use, and give everyone a chance to share, they can make every dinner a great dinner—not just because of the enjoyable food, but because of the enlightening conversations.

Make Family Dinnertime a Priority

We know a single mother with three teenage boys living at home. Her typical day starts at five-thirty in the morning when she gets up and prepares breakfast for her boys, who have early-morning classes. The boys get up and eat around six. During that time, their mom prepares sack lunches for them. Mom drops them off at school in time for their seven o'clock class and then hurries back home to get ready for work. She works from eight until five, and then it's back to the school at five to pick up the teenagers from sports practices. They all get home, and the teenagers quickly get ready for piano practice, karate, or Boy Scouts, all of which start at different times. Mom transforms into a chauffeur, driving one teenager one place and one to another until around eight. During the short breaks between activities, she prepares something for dinner. She picks up each teenager, and one by one they come home and devour their portion of dinner. It's now almost nine, and by then, this mother is exhausted!

This mom is not alone. The same schedule is played out in all different types of families. Families simply have so much going on during the day that we're lucky to even make dinner, let alone eat it together. For most families, eating together constitutes a special occasion reserved for a few Sundays, holidays, and maybe some cookouts during the summer.

All the extracurricular activities, sporting events, dance practices, and music performances are beneficial for teenagers' development. However, those beneficial activities sometimes crowd out other important and necessary activities such as family dinnertime. In order to make time for family dinners, families may need to rearrange schedules to accommodate this priority. We've found that establishing a regular time for family dinner helps. Dinnertime might be at five in the afternoon, it might be at eight at night, but the important thing is that dinnertime is together.

As your family strives to adjust to this new priority, don't get discouraged. It will take time for everyone in the family to rearrange his or her schedule. Make small, manageable goals that can help you obtain the larger goal of at least five family dinners a week. Your family could start with the goal of having family dinners at the same time during the weekend. Then, once you've accomplished that goal on a regular basis, you can move on to having family dinner a few nights during the week as well. Before too long, you'll be enjoying each other's company at least five times a week and experiencing the benefits that come from having a regular family dinnertime—benefits that are even more important than those gained from karate or Boy Scouts.

Not only will establishing a regular dinnertime benefit your teenagers now, but it will also benefit them in the future. Creating the habit in teenagers' lives now will make it easier for them to have regular dinnertime when they have children of their own.

Divide Dinner Responsibilities

One way to make sure family dinner happens daily is to divide responsibilities and share the work involved with making dinner between every family member. In many families, moms take the lead in preparing dinner every night. Moms are wonderful and seem to have superhuman strength and endurance, but even moms need help. Preparing dinner alone day after day will cause any mom unneeded stress. Luckily, every family member—especially teens—can help. Dinner doesn't have to be just Mom's responsibility.

When Jerrick lived at home, his family was as busy as they could be. He played volleyball, his three sisters danced, one of those sisters was into diving, one brother played basketball, the other brother played soccer, all were involved in music, and his youngest sister wanted to do everything her older siblings did. Even with all those activities, Jerrick's mom still found ways to involve all of her children in preparing dinner. Each child took turns helping Mom prepare dinner when they could. A few children were assigned to set the table, and a few were assigned to help Dad clean up after dinner. During some weeks, this method worked great. During other weeks, the method worked not-so-great. However, the family consistently tried to help in whatever way they could to get dinner on the table and have a few minutes together amid the chaos.

Jerrick may have griped back then about having to make dinner, but now he is grateful that his mom taught him how to cook a few dishes. He's pretty sure it was his cooking that originally attracted his wife to him. He may have complained about cleaning up after dinner, but now he is grateful that he knows how to clean his kitchen well. Jerrick remembers many times when he would be cleaning up dinner with his dad and they would start talking. These conversations would often carry on long after the dishes were clean and the countertops were washed.

As you assign dinner responsibilities to your teenagers, be an active participant with them as they try to fulfill their responsibilities. Teenagers will learn helpful life skills by preparing dinner, and the conversations you will have with your teenagers as you make and clean up dinner are just as valuable as the ones you have while eating.

Limit Technology Use

Using technology can be a great way for parents to connect with teenagers. Most teenagers use Facebook, Twitter, and Pinterest websites daily, so parents can learn much about their teenagers by being Facebook friends with them, following them on Twitter, or pinning something to their teenager's board on Pinterest. Most teenagers have cell phones; parents can communicate with teenagers by learning their digital language and sending a few text messages or starting a few Snapchats. But even with all the benefits of technology, it still doesn't replace good old face-to-face communication.

Texting only reproduces words, or verbal communication, onto a screen to be read by someone else. However, according to a study by Albert Mehrabian, verbal communication accounts for only 7 percent of what is being communicated in speech, while 93 percent is inferred by nonverbal communication.[3] Although the actual numbers can be debated, it's safe to say that much of what we say isn't just coming from our mouths, and in order to understand and connect with teenagers, we must get the entire message.

Jerrick remembers going to a restaurant and noticing a family there. Every individual family member was on some sort of electronic device. How sad that this family missed such a positive opportunity during that dinner because everyone was connecting digitally with people "out there" instead of connecting with each other "right here."

Brad remembers when he hosted a young man from out of state who had come for a summer conference at the university where Brad was teaching. The teenager stayed with the Wilcox family in their home. He was shocked when the family gathered for dinner and there was no TV on. "What do you do during dinner?" he asked.

"We talk. We visit. We catch up on everyone's day," Brad answered.

The young man exclaimed, "Whoa! That's awesome. In my house, we used to watch TV together, but then everyone fought about which show to watch, so now we usually just load up our plates and go watch TV in our own rooms." He liked eating with the Wilcoxes better.

When it comes to cooking dinner, technology helps, and you should use it. Look up new recipes or time saving tips. But when eating dinner, limit technology use. Have every family member, parents included, put away the technology during dinnertime. Try to limit answering phone calls to emergencies only. Set a rule of no texting at the dinner table. Turn off the TV, and turn on family communication.

Give Everyone a Chance to Share

After dinner is prepared, after phones have been put away, and after TVs have been turned off, dinner is served! The food at dinner will seem to taste better because every family member had a hand in its preparation (although make sure no one has a hand in the food itself). No dinner is complete without one final ingredient—communication.

When teenagers were asked when they would prefer to talk to their parents about something that's important to them, "nearly half of teens (47 percent) agree that during or after dinner is the best time."[4] There's something about a full stomach that makes everyone happy and encourages conversation. It is important during dinnertime to give everyone a chance to share in the conversation. Teenagers are all different. Some may be quiet compared to their other siblings, and some may enjoy talking and accidentally overshadow other voices, but parents can ensure that all have a say in the conversation because all have something to say.

Often, shy teenagers just need an opportunity to speak, and then it's difficult for them to stop! We have found some simple ways for parents to encourage conversation at dinner. A great way to find things to talk about is by going around the table and asking how each person's day went. As teenagers and parents share their day with each other, it brings the whole family closer together. Let the conversation continue and flow freely. Don't try to dictate the conversation to a desired goal. Simply listen to your teenagers, let them share what they are thinking, and respond to their needs as you discover them. If that doesn't work, here are a few sure-fire conversation starters:

- ○ Share something happening among extended family members—a cousin's graduation or an uncle's wedding.

- ○ Go around the table and let everyone respond to a "wh" question. If you could meet anyone, who would it be? If you had a superpower, what would you choose? If you could have a wish, what would it be?

- ○ Friendly debates can involve everyone. Avoid politics if that causes fights. Stick to topics like do you like the mountains or the ocean? Do you like a nice hotel or camping? Do you like movies or live theater?

- ○ Share memories. Everyone can talk about a favorite memory of a teacher, a family vacation, or a former house you lived in.

Sometimes a hedgehog won't come close to your hands to sniff them. When this happens, a brilliant idea is to place a tasty mealworm on the tips of your fingers to encourage the hedgehog over to you. Now, we aren't advocating bribery as an effective tool when it comes to communicating with teenagers, but some good food on the dinner table can encourage conversation. When we, as parents, make family dinnertime a priority, divide dinner responsibilities, limit technology use, and give everyone a chance to share, we can encourage our teenagers to open up and communicate. Communication between parents and teenagers at the dinner table can build confidence and familiarity between them just as a tasty treat can build confidence between you and a hedgehog. That's a wonderful way to connect.

Invitations to Action

How can you create meaningful dinner conversations with your teenager? Here are a few suggestions that can make a difference:

○ Bring your family together and discuss when a good time for family dinner would be each week. How will a regular family dinnertime benefit your teenager?

○ What responsibilities can you assign each teenager for dinner this week? How will those responsibilities benefit you and your teenager?

○ What communication skills can teenagers develop as they talk and listen during dinner? How can you help them develop those skills?

○ Think about the statistics presented in this chapter. Why do you think family dinners have such a big effect on a teenager's life? What effects have you seen or could you hope to see in your own home as you implement family dinnertime?

Endnotes:

1. "The Importance of Family Dinners IV." The National Center on Addiction and Substance Abuse at Columbia University. (New York: CASA Columbia, September 2007), i.

2. "The Importance of Family Dinners IV," 2.

3. Albert Mehrabian and Susan R. Ferris. "Inference of Attitudes from Nonverbal Communication in Two Channels." *Journal of Consulting Psychology* 31 (1967): 252.

4. "The Importance of Family Dinners IV," 11.

Chapter 4

Set Limits

B rad once had this conversation with a teenager he knows:
"I wish I could talk to my parents about the guy who came up to me and offered me drugs," the teen lamented.

"Have you ever tried talking to them about things like that?" Brad asked.

"Just once or twice, but nowhere near the number of times those things have happened to me."

"What keeps you from telling your parents what's really going on at school?"

"I don't know. I'm afraid they will get mad and blow up at me."

After the teenager shared more experiences about being uncomfortable talking to his parents, Brad finally asked, "What could your parents do to make you feel more comfortable talking to them?"

The teen responded, "I guess it's the attitude. They have to listen and try to understand. They could talk to me one-on-one instead of when other people are around."

Communicating with teenagers is like playing the piano. As many times as we can be shown how to play a song, we still have to finally put our hands on the keys and try. We can practice and prepare, but there still may be times during the actual recital when our minds go blank. We can be told how to communicate with teenagers over and over, but when a teenager wrecks the family car, all the training goes out the window. Suddenly, everything breaks down and we yell, "What's your problem? Why did you do that? When are you going to learn how to drive?"

Like learning to play the piano, communicating with teens takes patience, effort, and a lot of practice—especially when problems arise. Before becoming too discouraged with ourselves, we need to remember that even concert pianists have bad days now and then.

One parent asked us, "All this talk of love and caring is great, but what about when your teenager is out of line? What about when he has done something wrong? Aren't you supposed to have rules and maintain discipline?"

Teenagers need love, and they need standards. It is not an either-or situation. Expressing love freely provides a strong and secure foundation from which to enforce standards, and enforcing standards is really an evidence of love.

Some people find it easy to love without worrying about discipline. Others find it easy to discipline without love. It takes a lot of skill and personal integrity to combine them. It is no secret that, deep down, young people actually desire limits and boundaries. As much as they might say otherwise, they long for teachers and parents who can keep order. One fifteen-year-old girl said, "I am thankful for the standards and values my parents have given me. Other young people around me are not so lucky. I watch them, and they are not as happy as I am. I appreciate my parents for giving me high standards."

By setting limits, we offer teenagers the security, stability, and safety they need. But how do we do this without blocking communication? Here are some suggestions.

Set Clear Expectations

Teenagers need to know what is expected of them. Sixteen-year-old Micah said, "My parents teach me the black and white of things—no beating around the bush with them. They tell me exactly what they expect of me when it comes to my behavior. They teach me clearly and then say, 'You can choose to follow the rules or not, it's up to you, but you can't say you never knew the rules and the consequences for breaking them.'"

Most parents would say they do expect their children to obey. Often, however, they are only wishing for obedience because their expectations are not stated clearly and frequently to their children.

One fifty-year-old man hesitated when he was asked to do a presentation to teenagers, but finally he accepted the assignment. His supervisor brought him some materials and said, "Good luck. The last two presenters were eaten alive." The next day at work, after the man told a friend about his new assignment, the friend went out and bought a sympathy card and placed it on his desk.

When the man arrived home that evening, his wife said, "Don't let them get you discouraged. You have always worked well with the youth."

"Yes," he replied, "but that was when I was a lot younger than I am now."

On the day of the presentation, he was well prepared, and he greeted the teenagers cheerfully as they entered the room. But during the entire presentation, the teenagers acted as if he were not even there. They talked about school and told jokes, played with their cell phones, and when he tried to settle them down and get their attention, some of them were downright rude to him. He felt totally out of control.

He told his wife, "Those teenagers acted like complete hoodlums."

She listened to him describe the class and then asked, "Did they know where the fences were?"

"What do you mean?"

"It may sound strange," she said, "but I think teenagers are a lot like cows. They'll wander as far as they can and get into all kinds of trouble unless there is a fence. Once they know where the fences are, they are usually content to graze in the center of the field."

During the week, the man thought about this comment. He went to his next presentation prepared with his lesson and also with his fence. He greeted the young people as they entered the room and sat down, and then he said firmly, "While I present to you today, I expect you to listen, with no talking. If you have comments, please raise your hand and we'll hear them in turn. Put away your cell phones during my presentation. We are learning something important. It is essential that I have your attention."

What was the man's report to his wife after that presentation? Were the teenagers all wonderful? Did they all sit quietly with their hands folded nicely in their laps? Did everyone live happily ever after? No, but things went better than they had the week before. The fences that this man's wife mentioned are the clear expectations and limits we need to set for our teenagers. He told his wife, "I had to remind them to be quiet several times, and I had to wait and not continue until they were with me, but I made it through my presentation. Two girls even came up after and thanked me." It was a small, but crucial, victory.

Maintain Consistent Accountability

How many times do we state an expectation, or set a fence, but fail to follow through? We agree on a curfew with our teenagers, but then we let it slide when they don't make it in on time. We tell teenagers to listen, but then we keep on talking whether they are listening or not. Once we set an expectation, we must insist on getting the behavior we expect.

In Jerrick's home, his parents established a curfew when each child entered high school. The curfew was midnight, and each teenager knew the punishment if it were broken—Dad would scare him or her. It sounds silly, but it worked.

Like many teens, Jerrick tested the curfew to see if his parents would actually follow through on their threat. He thought, *My dad can't scare me*, but he would soon find out he was mistaken.

One night, Jerrick came home a little after midnight to find the porch light on and the front door still unlocked. He remembers thinking, *Everything looks normal. They must have forgotten or fallen asleep.*

Under that false sense of security, he walked confidently into his home, not knowing that his dad was hiding just behind the half wall bordering the front door. As Jerrick turned the corner, his father jumped up from behind the wall and grabbed his arm. Jerrick screamed in a high pitched tone he didn't know his teenage voice could still make and woke up several members of the household. The lesson was learned. Jerrick was never late again.

A few years later, Jerrick was home from college with some friends when his sister broke curfew. It was only by a few minutes, but the rule was maintained, and Jerrick and his friends happily helped Jerrick's dad scare his sister. Like Jerrick, she was never late again.

Express Appreciation Generously

One observant teenager said, "My parents are quick when it comes to punishing me for disobedience, but they are pretty slow to reward me whenever I do something right." When a teenager lives up to expectations, we must express our gratitude.

One father said:

> I never even thought of thanking my children for the little things they do. I guess I just expected them to do those things naturally. But I decided to try it. We had set a family goal to have less fighting, and I specifically asked the children to stop saying the words "stupid" and "shut up" to each other. Several days later, things were going pretty well. I went to each child to express my thanks for the use of better language in our home, and I couldn't believe the response. I thought they would think I was treating them like little babies. Instead, they were genuinely happy I had noticed their efforts. My teenage daughter even put a note in my car thanking me for being such a great dad.

Expressing appreciation not only shows teenagers that we appreciate their efforts, but it also provides motivation to continue positive behaviors. One of Jerrick's responsibilities as a child was mowing the lawn. "I remember my mother always complimenting me when I did a good job on the lawn," Jerrick says. "I felt good when she complimented me, so I wanted to continue mowing the lawn well because I knew it would make my mom proud of me, and in turn, I would feel proud of myself."

Correct in Private

When problems with teenagers occur, it is best to deal with them in private rather than before peers, brothers and sisters, or other adults. If we let ourselves get into power struggles with teenagers in front of others, we will likely lose. Most teenagers would sacrifice their relationship with us long before they would ever allow themselves to look weak in front of peers.

Seek a quiet time, such as just before bedtime. Pick a comfortable setting, one free from distractions or interruptions. In planning what to say, make sure that you have cooled down. Think of yourself as a consultant rather than a manager, a coach rather than a critic. Think of the conversation as an exploration rather than an accusation. Start by asking, "What happened?" or "What's wrong?" rather than, "I know you've been lying to me, and I want to know why."

Your teenager may say, "Nothing happened." Such a response is usually a test to see if you really care enough to ask again. Don't give up. Keep the conversation going or wait in silence. If you are still met with a blank stare or a "Not me," then continue asking questions. Inviting teenagers to speak is better than lecturing them.

Joy Saunders Lundberg wrote of one such time with her teenager:

> Our son came home from school one day and seemed discouraged. I said, "What's up? You seem down."
>
> He replied, "Jim [not his real name] is such a jerk."
>
> And I asked, "Oh, how's that?" I was surprised at what followed.
>
> "He's been inviting his girlfriend over to his house every day after school since his mom started working."

Resisting the temptation to expound a magnificent sermon on morality, I said, "Hmm."

And he said, "It's so stupid. He's just asking for trouble." Definitely similar to what I would have said, only more concise.

I asked, "What do you mean?" Then a flood of information poured forth regarding all the dangers of being alone in a house with a girlfriend. But it didn't stop there. He covered every base, including the terrible effects of venereal disease and abortion. All I did was listen and agree. I'm convinced he would have heard very little of the sermon had it been preached by me."[1]

Correcting in private allows us to help teenagers reflect on what has occurred ("What went well?" "What didn't go so well?"). We can guide them toward value judgments ("Is that helping you?"), and help them formulate a new goal or plan of action for the future ("What do you think we ought to do about it?"). In this way, we can stop having to play the role of the all-knowing dictator and simply start helping teenagers help themselves. Our job, as parents, is not to solve all of our children's problems for them, but rather to give them opportunities to begin solving their own problems.

If the situation requires discipline, remember that the word *discipline* comes from the word *disciple*, which means "a learner." Discipline, then, is teaching, training, and learning. It is not something we do to a child; rather, it is something we do *for* a child.

When giving direction, a concert pianist might say, "Just read the notes and play with gusto." This sounds simple enough. Still, when we try it, it just doesn't seem to work for us. We hit the wrong notes more often than we hit the right ones. But by working at it, we get better than we used to be. We may never play in any concert halls, but we might just hit the right notes in our homes where it matters the most. It's not enough to hit the right notes just once; we need to continue to practice in order to hit the right notes consistently.

The same is true when trying to hug a hedgehog. The hedgehog won't familiarize himself with your scent after just one try. He needs you to take off the gloves every time you try to hold him. The hedgehog expects your same scent, and gloves—or even a different perfume—can confuse him. When setting limits with teenagers, it's not enough to set those limits once, and we certainly don't want to confuse teenagers by continuously changing those limits. Instead, we can learn to regularly state expectations, maintain accountability, express appreciation, and correct in private. The biggest key is to keep trying. That counts in communication just as much as it counts in playing the piano and hugging hedgehogs.

Invitations to Action

How can you set appropriate limits for your teenager? Here are some keys that can help you think carefully about your choices:

- Think about what you expect from your teenager. How can you better communicate those expectations to your teenager?

- How do you hold your teenager accountable for his or her actions? What messages does your teenager get from you when you maintain accountability?

- During the past week, what has your teenager done that you appreciate? How can you express your appreciation?

- Think of a time when someone corrected you. What made it a positive or negative experience? What are some ways that you can help your teenager feel your love as you correct him or her?

Endnotes:

1. Joy Saunders Lundberg. "Helping Youth Choose Sexual Purity," *Ensign*, October 1991, 21.

Overcome Adversity

How to Hug a Hedgehog Rule #2

"Take your time; let him relax. If he rolls into a ball and extends his quills, stay calm and be patient."

A hedgehog faces many adversities in his life, ranging from natural predators to habitat destruction. When a hedgehog feels threatened, he rolls up, covering his soft underbelly and fully exposing his sharp quills. Teenagers also face adversity in their lives, but teenagers react to adversity in different ways. Here are four keys to help parents understand how they can help teenagers overcome adversity: talk to them about growing up and sex, help them confront their fears, be clear about reasons to avoid dangerous and unhealthy choices, and demonstrate to them how to learn from failures and setbacks.

Chapter 5

Talk about Growing Up and Sex

Looking back, all of us can probably remember times when we realized we were transitioning from childhood to young adulthood. For some, it may have been walking through high school doors for the first time and being engulfed in crowds of students, all clamoring to find their first-period classrooms. For others, it may have been that wonderful but yet strangely awkward feeling after a first kiss. It could be finally beating Dad at basketball, armed with newfound height, or maybe driving lessons with white-knuckled Mom in the passenger seat. Still, for others, it may have been answering the phone and having the person on the other end of the line comment, "Oh, sorry, you sound so much like your mom," or, "Wow, you answer the phone just like your dad."

All of us have growing-up memories because growing up is a natural part of life. Aside from when we were a newborn, our bodies experience the most growth during a time called puberty, a time when our childlike bodies transition to adulthood. Sometimes this transition goes quite smoothly, and other times teens experience growing pains, both literally and figuratively, as they try to navigate this new period of their lives. Mentioning the word *puberty* elicits a wide variety of emotions, from laughter to happiness to embarrassment, depending on the memories that surface.

When Jerrick thinks of puberty, one of the experiences he remembers happened during eighth grade. He was a member of his junior high's leadership council, and one of the council's responsibilities was reciting the Pledge of Allegiance and reading announcements over the intercom each morning. Members of the council would take turns performing this task, and Jerrick dreaded his turn, like most of his classmates. However, many of his classmates were afraid to read the announcements because they didn't want to slip up while reading. Jerrick was an advanced reader for his age and didn't worry as much about making mistakes as he did about having his voice crack during the announcements.

The first time Jerrick read the announcements, he walked down the hallway to the tech room thinking, *Voice, please don't crack. Please don't crack.* By the time he got to the door, he had talked himself into feeling pretty confident that things would go well. He opened the door and walked inside. The room seemed small, with a bunch of wires all over the place connecting this thingamabob to that whatchamacallit. There was a chair and a table with a microphone sitting on top of it in the far end of the room. He walked over to the table, sat down on the chair, and pulled out the sheet of paper he was given with the words he needed to say. He waited for the first period bell to ring, and once it was finished, he confidently pushed the on-air button on the microphone.

"Good morning, Brown Junior High School," Jerrick said. "Please staAAnd to recite the Pledge of Allegiance." Despite all the positive self-talk, Jerrick's voice cracked, right over the PA system.

The entire school heard it! Jerrick felt sure that his classmates were judging him and laughing at him. During the rest of the announcements (which, unfortunately, were really long that day), he was a nervous wreck and stumbled over his words many times. His voice cracked even more, adding additional insult to injury.

Brad had a similar experience growing up. He remembers getting taller and how his parents complained about having to keep buying new pants and shoes because he was growing so quickly. He remembers getting hungry and never feeling like he could get full. He welcomed the broadened shoulders he noticed in the mirror, but was mortified when he noticed his breasts getting a little larger and his nipples starting to stick out and become tender. He didn't know such changes were normal for growing boys. The only thing he could figure out was that he must be turning into his mother!

Experiences like Jerrick's and Brad's might be one reason actor and musician Rick Springfield, in an interview with Wendy Williams, humorously said, "Other than dying, I think puberty is about as rough as it gets."[1]

It's safe to say that most adults, when they look back on young adulthood, can all relate in one way or another to experiencing the pitfalls of puberty. However, puberty doesn't all have to be bad. Puberty can be navigated positively as teenagers experience new things, and parents can use puberty as a time to grow closer to preteens and teens. Parents can be trusted guides as children grow through puberty. Parents can seek accurate information, maintain open communication, and be direct when they speak to teens about growing up and sex. This gives teenagers the confidence they need to face puberty with a smile—even if that smile has braces on it.

Seek Accurate Information

Teenagers face staggering pressures and stress as they experience many social, emotional, and physical changes during puberty. For example, teenagers try to understand new attractions they may feel toward members of the opposite sex while simultaneously trying to deal with acne and body odors that may make them feel embarrassed in front of those same members of the opposite sex. They want others to know they are cool, but don't want to announce it because that's not cool. Secretly, they desire information about growing up and sex, but they don't want to admit they don't know as much as they wish they did. They need help, but they don't want to get it from their parents! We need to see through all that and take the lead. Some parents may see their teenagers' newfound interest in independence as a good thing when they willingly take on more responsibilities at home. Others see it as a bad thing when that independence leads to trouble at school.

As parents, we need to understand that the way we view our teenagers' experience with puberty will help determine teenagers' attitudes about puberty. If we focus only on the negative aspects of puberty, our teenagers are more likely to focus only on the negative. But when we focus on the positive, teenagers are more likely to focus on the positive as well. According to psychologist Dr. Marna Cohen and her colleagues, as parents gain knowledge about puberty and its effect on teenagers, parents are better equipped to focus on the positive instead of the negative.[2]

With knowledge comes increased perspective and patience when trying to glean the positives. With knowledge comes a greater capacity to love teenagers because we understand what they face. With knowledge comes a better ability to help teenagers when they face the negative aspects of growing up.

Parents already have more knowledge about puberty than they realize because they have already experienced growing up. But experiencing puberty and knowing how to explain puberty to a nervous, scared, and embarrassed twelve-year-old are entirely different matters. Gaining knowledge will help parents feel more calm and confident about explaining puberty to their children.

There are lots of resources available, but some provide information in a way that is complicated and technical. Others do so in a way that is crass and unrefined. Look for material that can provide information with an appropriate balance. The following list of resources may be helpful to you as you seek to learn more about puberty and about explaining puberty. Each website has helpful information, but make sure you take control of your own learning. Don't be afraid to deviate from their suggested discussion points. Don't disregard your beliefs and values, and find information that helps you translate those beliefs to your teenagers. Remember, every teen is different, and the tips these websites and books provide may not work for all. Find something that works for you and your family.

www.HHS.gov/ash/oah/resources-and-publications/info/parents/index.html

This government resource is a great starting point for parents who want to learn more about how to talk with teens about puberty and other adolescent topics. There are conversation tips and tools that will help you know the best way to initiate discussion with your teenagers.

www.NoPlaceLikeHome.org

No Place Like Home deals specifically with sex education in the home. The website allows you to select the specific age of your teenager to find topics that may relate to him or her at that time. They also have a book available for purchase if you prefer seeing information in print form.

www.AdvocatesForYouth.org/parents/

Advocates for Youth focuses on rights, respect, and responsibility. It is difficult for some parents to discuss puberty and sex with teens, but this website is filled with answers to some of the most common questions.

www.Familius.com/teenagers

Go to this website periodically to check for new insights from respected authors about puberty and other teenage issues.

Growing Up: Gospel Answers about Maturation and Sex by Brad Wilcox

This book is written so it can be read and understood by a child, and then discussed with parents. It presents information in a conservative religious context and helps define body terms and functions.

How to Talk to Your Child about Sex by Richard and Linda Eyre

This book focuses on how parents can discuss sex with their children of all different ages. It outlines talks that could be appropriate to have with children of a particular age, starting at age three and going up to age nineteen. Much of the book is formatted like a conversation, with suggestions for what parents might say, guesses at how children might respond, and follow-up questions.

Maintain Open Communication

Jerrick remembers that when he was in fifth grade, his teacher gave the class permission forms that parents needed to sign so their children could participate in an introductory sexual education presentation. Jerrick brought the form home, and his parents signed it. The night before the presentation, his parents took him out for dinner, leaving the rest of their kids home with a babysitter. During dinner, Jerrick's parents discussed what the class would be about. Although he doesn't remember much about the conversation, he does remember feeling his parents' love that night. He knew they knew. That made him feel comfortable instead of nervous. Such open conversation gave Jerrick the confidence that he needed to approach his parents with questions he had later during his teenage years.

Armed with knowledge, parents can confidently communicate with their teenagers about growing up and sex. Whether your child is ten or sixteen, it is never too late to establish and maintain open communication. The key is to start.

Discuss puberty with your children openly and honestly. While frankness is important in all the answers we provide, we should not resort to using gutter or slang terms in our discussions. Such terms communicate disrespect for our bodies and its functions. Using correct terms may take a little effort on our part, but we can become comfortable calling body functions and parts by their proper names.

A light and positive touch can make discussion easier. Too often, we unintentionally convey negative messages about our teenagers' bodies and sexuality with our tone of voice and our words. One father didn't exactly know how to respond when his teenage son asked him about AIDS. The dad finally said gruffly, "AIDS has to do with sex, so you don't have to worry about it."

The boy mustered his courage and said, "Well, what about sex?"

The father fidgeted nervously and blurted out an awkward answer, "Sex is something you shouldn't do."

As could be expected, this interchange closed the lines of communication instead of opening them. Surely grave mistakes can be made when sex is engaged in inappropriately or in promiscuous and unhealthy ways. However, this father unthinkingly conveyed a negative message about sex, even in marriage, to his young son. If we are not careful, our teenagers can get the idea that their bodies are ugly and that sex is dirty or bad no matter what. We must try to express ourselves in positive ways when discussing sex and other aspects of puberty.

Talk Directly

During puberty, teenagers become aware of the immense capacity their bodies have to love, both emotionally and physically. This new awareness will result in questions—both spoken and unspoken—that need to be answered by parents. Schools, friends, advisors, teachers, and others should never substitute for parents in teaching children about sexuality and maturation. One study found that teens whose parents discussed sex with them honestly and openly were more likely to put off having sex until a more mature time in their lives, such as marriage.[2] In fact, most teenagers would prefer to talk to their parents about sex rather than teachers or friends.[3] Teens trust parents because they know parents are invested long-term and have their best interests at heart. They also know that parents can convey the facts in the context of family values and standards—something teachers, friends, and the media can't do as effectively.

Talking to teenagers about sex can feel awkward at first, but it's important. Some awkwardness can be avoided if we talk to teenagers about sex in private. Even a family setting may be too public to be able to meet the needs of everyone gathered without embarrassing some and overwhelming others. Personal conversations allow us to teach more sensitively and effectively. If teens do not initiate discussions, we must look for appropriate opportunities to bring up the subjects ourselves. Having "the talk" is not a one-time experience. Often, the subject of sex needs to be first discussed during the pre-teen years and then revisited many times throughout the teenage years. Each teenager is different, but we should not be afraid to discuss sexual topics with teenagers whenever we feel that discussion is needed.

Some parents worry that by speaking frankly with their teens about their bodies and sex, they are somehow promoting or condoning promiscuous behavior. In fact, the opposite is true. Our experience has shown us that the most sexually active teens are usually the least informed. Silence and ignorance, not open communication, often lead to poor choices by teenagers. The more solid sexual information teens gain from their parents, the more capable they are of making mature choices. The results of one national survey showed that 88 percent of teens delayed sexual experiences because of frank and direct discussions with parents.[4]

We need to be careful not to overload teenagers, and especially preteens, with more information than they really need or want. We know of one mother whose six-year-old asked, "Where did I come from?" When the mother launched into an oration on the facts of life, the little girl interrupted, "All I asked is where I came from. My friend Stephanie says she came from Omaha."

The surest way to estimate just how much teenagers know or want to know is to ask probing questions. For example, when a young teenage boy says, "I just don't understand girls," a parent could ask, "Why? What do you mean?"

A teenage girl remarks, "My friend Johnny is acting weird around me, and I don't know why." Her mother could ask, "How is he acting weird?"

If a teenager asks, "What does contraceptive mean?" a parent could respond, "I would love to answer that question, but first, when did you hear that word?"

Probing questions are not an attempt to change the subject or avoid giving a straight answer. Rather, they offer a chance to listen as well as speak—to gather enough information so that parents can respond to their teenagers' needs effectively.

Once parents have determined what a teenager knows and what he or she still needs to learn, they must not hesitate to say what needs to be said. As parents, we need to be factual, honest, and direct, even when we feel uneasy. It's OK to answer questions by saying, "I don't know everything, but I'll do my best," or "You know, I'm not quite sure about that. Let's find out together." Willingness to talk to our teenagers, despite uneasiness, will strengthen teens' confidence in us.

Sometimes, when you attempt to pick up a hedgehog for the first few times, the hedgehog rolls into a ball and extends his quills. When this happens, patience and persistence is required. Eventually, the hedgehog will warm up to you. As time passes, he will become easier to handle. Similarly, as parents play an active role in helping teenagers navigate puberty, teenagers will warm up to them. When parents gain knowledge about the process their teenagers are undergoing, when they maintain open lines of communication, and when they explain sexual topics with directness, they can connect with their teenagers and help them approach and survive puberty with a positive attitude.

Invitations to Action

How can you positively talk to your teenager about growing up and sex? Here are a few suggestions that can help:

- o Think of a time when you were taught about growing up and sex. What were some aspects of that experience that worked well for you? Some that didn't? How can you make "the talk" and the talks that will follow more positive experiences for your teen or preteen?
- o Make a list of words that describe body parts and functions (such as *genitals* or *intercourse*). How can you explain those words to your teen in a respectful way and also in a way that he or she can understand?

Endnotes:

1. Lauri Bedigian, "Rick Springfield Talks with Wendy." *Examiner.com*, October 20 2010. http://www.examiner.com/article/rick-springfield-talks-with-wendy.

2. Marna Cohen, et al., "Parental Reactions to the Onset of Adolescence." *Journal of Adolescent Healthcare* 7 (1986): 101–106.

3. Michael D. Resnick, "Protecting Adolescents from Harm: Findings from National Longitudinal Study on Adolescent Health." *Journal of American Medical Association*, 278 (1997): 823–32.

4. Karen A. Hacker, "Listening to Youth: Teen Perspectives on Pregnancy Prevention." *Journal of Adolescent Health*, 26/4 (2000): 279–88.

5. Laura Bell, "Let's Talk About Sex." *Reader's Digest*, March 2008.

Chapter 6

Face Your Worst Fear

"What is your worst fear?" Brad once asked his children.

"Bees!" answered his oldest daughter immediately. That was a predictable answer after her encounter with an unfriendly swarm at a picnic a few years earlier. She had been stung more than twenty times.

His fifth-grade son admitted he was "a little" afraid of sharks. He had seen them only in movies, but that was close enough for him.

His four-year-old daughter said, "Daddy, I don't like the big booms in the sky." Of course, she was describing thunder.

Brad turned to his youngest son and asked, "Are you afraid of anything?"

His eyes got big, and he nodded his head vigorously.

"What is your worst fear?" Brad probed.

He squared his little shoulders, stuck out his chin, put his hands on his hips, and declared, "Vacuums!"

Now that Brad's children are grown, their fears have changed. After all, we don't know many teenagers who can't handle bees and thunder. Most teenagers aren't terrified of sharks—especially if they don't live near an ocean. And can you imagine a star football player being interviewed after the state championship game and admitting he is afraid of vacuums?

So what are teenagers' worst fears? One study was conducted in which parents were asked to name their children's worst anxieties. A few anxieties that were named included nuclear war, terrorism, being kidnapped, and the possibility of parents getting divorced. When teenagers were asked the same question, the worst anxieties that surfaced were very different from what their parents had assumed. Teenagers were most afraid of not having enough friends, being teased or bullied, and being embarrassed in front of their peers. The study reported that the teenagers surveyed actually feared humiliation in front of peers more than they feared having to undergo surgery.[1]

Although teenagers may not admit it openly, the results of the study are pretty much on target. Persecution from peers is a serious pressure. One mother wrote the following letter about her teenage daughter (whom we'll call Brittany):

> We are having some anxious moments with Brittany. We have spent much of the school year wondering what tricks she will pull next. They aren't your usual teenage acts of rebelliousness. They are mischievous and quite out of the ordinary. We have talked to her, and she knows our expectations. Brittany has even tearfully said that she wants to try to be better. But she has a friend who seems to have total control over her. Whenever there is trouble, this friend is not just in the middle of it; she is the

instigator of it. And Brittany just goes along with anything her friend suggests.

It turns out that one day Brittany's friend suggested they skip school and go to Brittany's home, since her parents were gone. They brought several other teenagers to the house and had a party, including beer and boys, and you can figure out the rest. Brittany's dad, for some reason, decided to come home in the middle of the day to pick up something. His arrival was quite a surprise for the teenagers at his house. They scrambled to get out and left behind an awful mess, but at least Brittany's dad was able to stop the party before it went any further.

When Brittany's parents later confronted her about it, she cried. She knew it was wrong and against their household rules. She sincerely had not wanted to do it. Through her sobs, she confessed, "I just didn't know what else to do. I was afraid of what my friends would say to everyone if I refused to go along with them." Brittany explained to her parents that her friend had "forced" her into it and "made" her do it. Had her friend held her at gunpoint? No. The friend had used a different weapon: negative peer pressure.

Brittany's mother concluded her letter by saying, "Brittany's need for acceptance by her friends and her desire to be popular with the boys are consuming her." This mother was right. Even Brittany knew it, but what could she do? How can Brittany and other teenagers face and conquer this "worst fear"? Here are a few keys that might help us unlock and confront these worst fears in teenagers.

Expect the Best

Teenagers need to realize that other people aren't usually paying as much attention to them as they think. Most teenagers are simply too worried about themselves to really spend much time analyzing others. At a dance, teenagers may worry about whether their hair is in place, their clothes are just right, and their dance moves fit in. All the while, those around them are usually so worried about their own hair, clothes, and dance moves that they're not even noticing others.

In the middle of Brad's sophomore year, his high school announced auditions for the annual Shakespearean play. *This is great!* he thought. He pictured himself in a colorful Elizabethan costume playing a rousing role, and he got all worked up. Between American History and lunch, he picked up a tryout sheet in the office.

As the afternoon passed, Brad began to reconsider. After all, what would his peers say if they found out he wanted to be in a Shakespearean play? It was easy for him to imagine the hateful names they might call him. Still, when school ended, he mustered all his courage and joined the audition line forming in the C-wing stairwell. The other students around him appeared to be all juniors and seniors. Brad began to panic. *What if they think my audition is terrible?* he thought. In his mind, he could picture them laughing and whispering cruel things behind his back. He envisioned himself on stage, dodging all the pencils, spit wads, shoes, rocks, and desks that they would probably throw. He thought, *What are you doing? You're going to look like a fool.* Quickly, he turned from the audition line and walked away.

At dinner that evening, Brad only ate one taco instead of his usual three, so Brad's dad realized something was on his mind. "What's up?" he asked.

"I want to try out for a play, but they won't let me."

"Who won't?" his dad asked.

"You know. They."

"Who are they?" Brad's dad asked again.

"The kids at school," he answered in exasperation. "You know, peer group, the older students, the popular people." He fumbled for some specific names, but couldn't think of a single one.

Then, with the infallible wisdom of most fathers, Brad's dad explained that as people mature, it becomes less and less important what other people think or say. It took him a while to finally convince Brad that he was the only one stopping him from doing what he wanted to do.

Before bed that night, Brad rescued the wrinkled tryout sheet from the pocket of his jeans and read it over again. He thought of the students in line for the auditions. They were probably just as nervous as he was. They were probably too nervous about their own performances to criticize his. He knew auditions were going on until the end of the week, so he promised himself that the following day he would not allow himself to be intimidated out of his intentions. He would try out.

Well, that's just what Brad did, and guess what? No one laughed. He even got a part in the play.

Hear the Hidden Messages

Some teenagers might think, *Well, maybe no one laughed at you, but they would have laughed at me.* One young woman told us, "One of my friends watches me like a hawk. She's always bugging me, cutting me low, or making some rude remark about the way I talk or dress. If she doesn't say it to me, she says it behind my back."

Do you think your teenagers have ever felt watched like that? We often overhear teenagers say, "I don't dance," "I don't play sports," or "I don't speak in public." Usually it's because, when they have tried in the past, someone has laughed at their awkward attempts. It is important to teach teenagers to expect the best and help them realize that most people aren't going to tease, but there are always a few people who enjoy being the exception to any rule. When those characters start to torment and belittle, we need to help our teenagers hear the hidden message—not just the obvious message coming out of bullies' mouths, but the less obvious message behind those words.

We've seen speakers in meetings look so frightened that we've wanted to rush to the phone and call 9-1-1 before they fall over dead. Yet those same speakers usually begin their addresses with something like, "I'm so happy to be here" or "I'm thankful for this opportunity." On such occasions, isn't it pretty easy to see the message behind their words coming through loud and clear?

The same is true when peers ridicule, intimidate, or exclude other teenagers. When teens intimidate or bully others by posting mean or offensive words on Facebook, perhaps the bullies really desire friendship and acceptance but don't know how to achieve their desires. The hidden message behind those actions is that those teenagers don't feel good about themselves. When cut-lows and rude comments by peers hurt teenagers, helping those teenagers hear the hidden message behind the hurtful actions can soften the blows and help teens stay positive and keep a broader perspective.

Act with Confidence

Author Victor Harris told of how his small son, McKay, participated with four of his friends in putting one of the neighborhood cats in the freezer. His father sent him to his room to think about how he might have handled the situation differently. You see, the boy loved animals and was normally very sensitive to them, but he did not want to lose face in front of the friends who had dared him to freeze the feline.

Mr. Harris wrote, "A few weeks later, we were grateful when he stood up against peer pressure. . . . One of his friends had a lighter and proposed using it to burn an earthworm. McKay jumped in, grabbed the worm, and, holding it up in the air, declared, 'You're not going to burn this worm!'"[2]

One teenager offers this advice to her peers: "If your friends start making fun of you, don't wimp out and crawl off into a corner. Hold your head up! Inside, you may be dying, but keep doing what you are doing. As long as you know that what you are doing is right, act as if what they are saying doesn't matter one bit because it really doesn't." Easy to say, but does she actually follow her own advice?

Yes, she does. Once, she saved her own money to buy a top she really liked. She wore it to school, only to have a friend greet her and say, "I can't believe you're wearing that. It's ugly!"

When the girl got home after school, she took off the brand-new top, shoved it in the bottom of her closet, and decided never to wear it again. Then she thought, *Wait! What am I doing? I like this. I spent my own money for it. Since when do I let my friends dress me?* The girl grabbed her top, washed it, removed the wrinkles, and wore it again—often.

We've seen other teenagers act with similar confidence. Brad remembers chaperoning a youth dance where he saw several teenagers begin dancing like chickens. Others saw them, too, and began to laugh. The teenagers heard the laughter but kept right on dancing. In fact, they were so—pardon the pun—cocky, that some of the others at the dance started joining them. It was not long before half the teenagers in the gym were dancing like chickens.

Replace Fear with Hope

During his freshman year of high school, Jerrick tried out for the freshman volleyball team. By his own admission, he wasn't very good, but he made the team anyway. It was a large team—so large that he was rarely allowed to play during scrimmages in practice, let alone play in an actual game. It was quite a surprise to him when his number was called to sub in for a teammate during one game. "I was scared," Jerrick remembers. "My parents were there. My siblings were there. All my friends were on the team, and I didn't want to let anyone down."

It didn't matter that the team was dominating its opponent. It didn't matter that there was no possible way for Jerrick to cause his team to lose the game. He was scared because of what everyone around him would think if he didn't play well. One of Jerrick's worst fears in high school was disappointing others, and although he can't remember exactly how he played that night, he remembers perceiving their disappointment.

As high school progressed, Jerrick worked at his volleyball skills so much that he eventually found himself as one of the varsity leaders and a starter on the team. More importantly, he had gained confidence—confidence in his skills and confidence in himself. That's the type of confidence that doesn't rely on other people's thoughts, words, or deeds, but rather on the positive thoughts, words, and deeds of self. His team played many times that season, and Jerrick didn't get scared anymore. He would walk onto that court with excitement. He had replaced fear with hope.

As a senior, one of Jerrick's favorite activities was to go help the freshman team warm up before their games. He could see himself in some of those younger players. He could see their fear and lack of self-confidence, but he reminded them to have hope. With hard work, they could overcome their fears and eventually be great players. He knew it because he'd done it himself. He wanted to help those freshmen have hope in their own potential.

Bees? Sharks? Thunder? Vacuums? What is your teenager's worst fear? Maybe, deep down, it has something to do with facing rejection, humiliation, and embarrassment before his or her peers. When people pick on them, tempt them, or push them to the limit, help teenagers remember they are not the only ones to face such persecution and negative pressure. They can act with confidence and replace their fear with hope.

Fear is the main reason a hedgehog will roll into a ball and extend his quills. That action is a defense mechanism for the hedgehog, but as he senses that whatever was causing his fear has departed, he relaxes. It is easiest for you to hug a hedgehog when he is relaxed. It is easiest to connect to teenagers when they are relaxed and comfortable rather than afraid. As we strive to connect with teenagers, we must address their very real fears because, as parents, we are in the best position to help our teenagers overcome them. Expecting the best, hearing the hidden messages, acting with confidence, and replacing fear with hope are four keys that parents can use to help teenagers face fears. Perhaps one of your worst fears is not being able to connect effectively with your teenager—but just by reading this you're working on overcoming that fear. Just as it is possible for you to overcome your fears, it's possible for teenagers to overcome theirs as well.

Invitations to Action

How can you help your teenager overcome his or her fears? Here are some points to ponder:

○ Does your teenager expect positive outcomes? If not, how can you encourage a different attitude? What personal experiences could you share?

○ What are the hidden messages your teenager receives when he or she feels rejection or negative pressure? How can you bring those hidden messages to light?

○ Does your teenager have strong self-confidence? How can you help improve his or her inner confidence?

○ What are your fears, and how have you replaced them with hope? How can your teenager learn from your example? What other role models could you introduce to your teens?

Endnotes:

1. James Lincoln Collier, "What Your Child Fears Most." *Reader's Digest*, October 1988, 7–12.

2. Victor Harris, *Sharing the Light*. Salt Lake City: Deseret Book, 1993.

Chapter 7

Remember What's *Not* on the Warning Labels

"Warning: What you are about to drink or smoke can kill you!" Such labels appear on cans of beer and packages of cigarettes everywhere, and yet teenagers continue to use these products with alarming frequency. One prominent study reports that marijuana use among high school seniors is as high as 22 percent,[1] and another study states that 50 percent of all high school seniors reported using alcohol in the past month.[2]

Apparently it's not enough to know that alcohol is linked to disorders of the nervous system, memory loss, cirrhosis of the liver, heart and kidney disease, loss of vision, gastric disturbances, excessive bowel activity, low immunity, and malnutrition. Obviously it means little that smoking causes cancer of the lungs, lips, tongue, and mouth, as well as heart disease, chronic bronchitis and emphysema, circulatory problems, high blood pressure, and peptic ulcers, and that using marijuana causes brain damage. If those who produce alcohol, tobacco, and other harmful substances were required to list all the dangers of using their products, the warning labels would completely cover every can, bottle, pack, and carton.

Still, it appears that some teenagers think such inevitable health problems will never happen to them. They say, "I'm different," "I can handle it," and "I'll beat the odds." Even if they are lucky enough to postpone health problems for a few years, their lives are still endangered by the way smoking and drinking impairs their ability to operate vehicles, erodes their good judgment, and gives a false sense of bravado that leads to violence—no small consideration in these days of armed gangs.

With so many negative consequences, why do young people choose to smoke and drink? They can't really buy into the ridiculous lyrics of songs on the radio that say in essence, "I know this stuff will kill me, but what a way to go." Maybe they believe the clever and deceitful advertisements that try to convince us life is not complete without using substances that cause regular vomiting. Perhaps teenagers just have money to burn (the stuff is expensive) or are just kidding themselves into believing that smoking and drinking are "no big deal." (After all, can a product that sponsors Olympic athletes and has the best Super Bowl commercials be all that bad?) One teenager said to us, "I figure it can't be too dangerous or they wouldn't let it be legal for adults." Such reasoning obviously makes our point—these products can cause brain damage. Part of helping teenagers overcome adversity is communicating warnings of real dangers in their lives.

To do so, we must go beyond the warnings on labels informing teenagers of the physical consequences of using harmful substances and focus on other consequences as well—the serious emotional and social consequences that never show up on any of the warning labels. Still, they are as real and frightening as any cancer or car accident. Parents must inform their teenagers of these consequences because the people pushing for teens to try those substances surely won't. When communicated with love, these warnings from parents can outweigh peer pressure to consume these harmful products.

Warning: Drinking and Smoking Deprive You of Your Ability to Choose

When Jerrick was working with a concrete company, he noticed that many of his fellow workers took several five-minute breaks during the course of the day to smoke their cigarettes. One worker even told him that he smoked two packs of cigarettes a day. The worker said he started smoking because it calmed his nerves, but after he started, he couldn't stop. He had tried unsuccessfully to stop many times. What started out as a choice to smoke turned into a constant desire over which he has little control. Even though he wants to quit, that desire isn't enough to break the hold the cigarettes have on him. His smoking doesn't free him, as he originally thought. It binds him.

Teenagers must understand that our right to choose for ourselves is inhibited when we use substances that are habit-forming. When Brad taught sixth grade, one of his students drew a poster that won a statewide contest. This student had simply drawn a hand in chains, with the links of the chain made of cigarettes. The caption said, "Smoking makes you a slave." Every sixth grader needs to understand that message.

One teenager said, "But I can stop whenever I want. I've quit lots of times before." Did he even realize how silly he sounded? If he had really quit all those times, why was he still doing it?

Another teenager said, "I'm not hooked. I can quit right now." When challenged to prove it, the teenager lasted a whole twenty minutes.

Warning: Drinking and Smoking Lower Self-Esteem

After winning his second NBA championship, a popular basketball player was photographed during the victory parade a few days later smiling with his teammates and smoking a very large, expensive, Cuban cigar.[3] When teenagers see that image, what do they think? They see a happy, smiling "role model" smoking and think that if they also smoke, they'll experience happiness and success as well. In reality, the happiness came from that athlete's goal setting and hard work to reach those goals, not the cigar in his mouth.

The smiles we see in the ads (usually on the faces of models and athletes who often avoid the stuff they are paid to promote) certainly don't indicate low self-esteem. However, most teenagers who engage in drinking or smoking are really just searching for a way to camouflage their poor self-images and find acceptance and approval. Those who don't feel cool, strong, and popular must seek desperately for ways to appear cool, strong, and popular. Sadly, once the cigarettes, joints, and drinks are finished, feelings of self-esteem have gone up in smoke, and young people feel as empty as the crumpled, discarded beer cans. Confidence doesn't come from a can. It comes from knowing "I can." Teenagers (or anyone for that matter) won't feel good about themselves from lighting up. For teenagers, high self-esteem comes from striving to reach their potential.

Warning: Drinking and Smoking Diminish Ambition

Teenagers need to understand that when someone becomes so focused on how and where to get the next supply, when the next party is happening, and how to avoid the police, there is little time and energy left for pursuing positive goals. Grades plummet. Extracurricular activities evaporate. Good job opportunities disappear. Future dreams are severely limited.

As a sixth-grade teacher, Brad always asked his students what they wanted to be when they grew up. They all dreamed of being professional athletes, dancers, movie stars, astronauts, doctors, lawyers, teachers, and good moms and dads. "You can do it!" he encouraged them. "You can do anything!" One boy told him often of his goal to become an airline pilot. This boy talked constantly about flying and could name all the different types of airplanes by heart. Imagine Brad's sadness when he found out a few years later that the boy had become involved with smoking, drinking, and drug abuse. He eventually dropped out of high school. It looks like there will be one less airline pilot in the world and one less dream fulfilled. On the other hand, as we help teenagers avoid using harmful and addictive substances, we can help their ambition maintain enough altitude to soar toward their dreams.

Warning: Drinking and Smoking Start a Downward Spiral

We rarely hear of someone drinking and smoking without also hearing other risky behavior mentioned in the same stinky breath. It may be shoplifting, lying, pornography, drug abuse, gang activity, or unhealthy sexual choices. Other problems such as depression—and, in some cases, even suicide—can be unwanted results of a downward spiral started by smoking and drinking.

This downward trajectory carries teens away from the people who love them and could help them most. One particular young man talked to Jerrick recently about his addiction to alcohol. He said, "My family doesn't drink, but they all know that I do. I hardly ever go home anymore because I know they judge me." In reality, his family still loves him, even though he's involved with this addictive behavior. However, this young man perceives that he's being judged, and because of that perception, he stays away from the very people who could help him.

When young people smoke and drink, they often feel so self-conscious that they lose their desire to participate in wholesome activities. They often become withdrawn, irritable, defensive, and even hostile. Perhaps one of the worst consequences of smoking and drinking is that it often keeps those who need help the most from reaching out and seeking that help. They are like sick patients refusing to see a doctor. "I can handle it on my own" is a phrase parents hear over and over again from young people who wander farther and farther from parents, counselors, and teachers who can truly offer the help and support they need.

Warning: Drinking and Smoking Limit Your Friendships

During junior high school, Jerrick and a good friend enjoyed going to the park, playing basketball, and walking home from the bus stop together. However, things began to change once they entered high school. This friend began drinking, smoking, and using marijuana. With his new habits, his attitude began to change. He became less social, and the activities that attracted him became increasingly risky. Although Jerrick was willing to continue being friends with him, the other boy no longer wished to associate with Jerrick. The friend's desires had changed. He was exchanging real friends for substances and crowds that were a poor substitute in the long run.

Teenagers need to understand that every sip of beer and every puff on a cigarette or joint means fewer bright, intelligent, and healthy-minded individuals that teenagers can call friends. Soon, those who smoke and drink are limited—not only by bad physical habits, but also by the impression (real or perceived) that their circle of friends can grow no larger than those who share their same addictions.

Warning: Drinking and Smoking Can Break Your Parents' Hearts

"It's my life, and it's my body," said one young woman. "Who cares what I do?" When a child makes poor choices, the disappointment, frustration, and failure felt by parents is overpowering. Teenagers need to know that the pain of their poor choices will be felt intensely by those of us who take our roles as parents seriously. They need to know that it's not quite as easy as people think for some of us to brush aside experimentation with harmful substances with such comments as "Boys will be boys," "Everyone does it," or "Maybe it's just a phase; she'll grow out of it."

Everyone has heard the old saying that you can count the seeds in an apple, but you can't count the apples in a seed. In the same way, we believe teenagers must understand that you can count the drops of beer in a can or bottle, but you can't count the tears caring parents will shed if their children make poor choices. You can weigh the amount of tobacco or marijuana you consume, but you can't weigh the private grief felt by dedicated parents whose children throw away their futures.

It Is Possible to Quit

Focusing on emotional and social consequences, as well as physical ones, when warning teens will offer them validation for their healthy choices and continued motivation to resist peer pressure to drink, smoke, and engage in other risky behaviors. However, those who have struggled need to also hear words of hope that can spark a desire to change, seek help, break bad habits, and begin anew. It is possible.

Jerrick has a friend named Jerry who decided to quit smoking. He worked construction and used cigarettes as a way to combat the stress that comes along with that job, but he realized it was an unhealthy habit. He had quit drinking many years before and felt sure that he had the capacity to kick smoking as well. Still, no matter how hard he tried, he just couldn't seem to do it for many years.

Finally, he and his wife decided to quit together. They tried patches but realized that they weren't just addicted to the nicotine; they were addicted to the way holding a cigarette kept their hands busy. They missed always holding something, so they looked outside the box for a solution. Along with the patches, they carried cinnamon sticks around with them and sucked on the sticks. Eventually, they could go longer periods of time without the patches or the sticks, and now they don't rely on either. They are completely free of their addiction.

Harry Hale Russell, Brad's great-grandfather, was a heavy smoker until later on in his life. That was back in the days when men carried around small sacks of tobacco and rolled their own cigarettes. His wife was extremely concerned when, after much prodding from herself and others, he was still rolling cigarettes and smoking. In fact, he smoked right up until the day he had promised to quit once and for all. Then, that was the end. He had determined he would never use tobacco again, and he never did.

"It wasn't easy for him," Brad's grandmother told him when he was growing up. "He had smoked for over twenty years." Brad's grandma remembered her father always kept one sack of tobacco on his dresser. When he felt tempted, he would stare at that sack and ask himself, "Which is stronger, you or me?" Brad's grandmother said, "My father quit smoking because he knew it was best for him and for his family. When he knew something was best, he was uncompromising."

A hedgehog rolls into a ball because he understands and correctly interprets the warning signs of approaching danger. He chooses not to expose his soft underbelly to something that might end up being harmful to him. A hedgehog has instincts that tell him what is dangerous, but teenagers need to be taught some of the dangers of substance abuse, as well as the benefits that come when they choose not to participate in unhealthy lifestyles. Those who decide not to smoke or drink will experience wonderful benefits in their lives. Along with improved health, they will be able to feel emotions, safeguard their ability to choose, improve feelings of self-worth, pursue positive goals, broaden friendships, strengthen family ties, avoid additional problems, and bring happiness to others. As teenagers come to understand the keys to and benefits of a healthy lifestyle, they can gain motivation to roll up into a ball of quills and protect themselves from the pitfalls of smoking and drinking by making wise decisions to heed those warning signs.

Invitations to Action

How can you warn teenagers of the consequences that come from smoking, drinking, and other harmful activities? Here are a few ideas to think about:

- How can you communicate the importance of making right choices with your teenager? How did people effectively communicate that to you?

- Since a positive self-image helps teenagers resist peer pressure, what ways can you help your teenager develop greater self-esteem?

- Think of families you know in which drinking and smoking have put a strain on family relationships. How can you help teens learn from these experiences?

- Consider friends in your own life who have lifted you up or pulled you down. How can you help your teenager see the importance of developing and maintaining good friendships?

- How can you support someone you know who is struggling with an addiction? If it is your teenager, what ways can you sustain his or her resolve to quit?

Endnotes:

1. "Drug Facts: High School and Youth Trends," National Institute on Drug Abuse, January 2014. http://www.drugabuse.gov/publications/drugfacts/high-school-youth-trends.

2. Bridget M. Kuehn, "Shift Seen in Patterns of Drug Use Among Teens," *The Journal of the American Medical Association*, 295/6 (2006): 612–613

3. "Photos: Miami Heat 2013 NBA Championship Victory Parade." *The Denver Post*, June 24, 2013. http://photos.denverpost.com/2013/06/24/photos-miami-heat-2013-nba-championship-victory-parade/.

Chapter 8

Learn from Failure

Believe it or not, some roofs aren't as sturdy as they may seem. While working construction, Jerrick learned this lesson the hard way.

When he was home from college during summer break, Jerrick took on a demolition job. The job seemed simple (and fun) enough: tear out parts of a house in preparation for a major remodel. Maybe it was the relative simplicity of the job, or maybe it was the need for extra money, but whatever the reason, he decided to do as much of the job as he could by himself.

There was a covered porch in the backyard that needed to be demolished. The roof of this particular porch was built using plywood and 2x6 pieces of wood attached to the main roof with a layer of shingles on top. It also happened to be fifty years old, so the structural integrity of the roof wasn't the best. Let's just say it wouldn't pass any sort of housing inspection nowadays.

Jerrick decided to climb onto the roof and tackle this particular project from the top down. He recalls:

"I remember thinking that I needed to be careful. The roof looked pretty sturdy, but it was old, so you just never know what can happen. I tried to make sure I only stepped where there was a 2x6 supporting my weight, but I must have missed one. I was bending over to start ripping those shingles off, and all of a sudden the roof caved in right underneath me. I fell, but caught myself by my armpits and pulled myself back up. My shins and sides were all scraped up from the fall and the climb back up."

Robert Burns once said, "Even the best laid schemes of mice and men often go awry."[1] Although Jerrick planned to be careful, things still went wrong. In teenagers' lives, sometimes their best goals and aspirations go unfulfilled; sometimes they make a wrong step and fall. What happens in those situations? How can we help our teenagers learn from goals that aren't reached? How can we help them learn from their mistakes? These aren't simple questions, and the answers vary from teen to teen, but we can teach teenagers to look for positive lessons, to accept responsibility, to maintain a positive attitude, and to reassess their goals.

Look for Positive Lessons

Negative experiences don't have to have negative lessons associated with them. In fact, negative experiences are often when teenagers can learn positive lessons.

Many people desire dogs, cats, or hamsters as pets, but not Jerrick. Sure, a dog is his first choice for a pet, but he and his wife love teacup pigs. Unfortunately, these adorable pigs are costly and not very suitable for apartments, but dreams are free. Maybe one day they'll get to see a teacup pig up close; however, there's one type of "pig" Jerrick never wants to meet again—the swine flu.

After celebrating a friend's birthday by eating dinner with him at a Mexican restaurant, Jerrick noticed he was shivering and felt a little cold. This was pretty common for him. Jerrick often gets cold in public places, especially restaurants, but this time was unusual. The shivers increased as he pulled into the driveway of his home. Once there, even his nice warm bed couldn't stop the shivers. Jerrick battled with the shivers all night, but the shivers won. Jerrick woke from his restless sleep with a cold sweat on his forehead and a burning in his hands and toes. He knew he needed help.

Jerrick spent the next few days in front of his fireplace curled up in a comfy armchair looking out through his window overlooking the Columbia River in Eastern Washington. Under different circumstances, that might have been utterly relaxing, but unfortunately, he also spent those next few days waiting for his 104 degree temperature to subside. Instead of enjoying a nice Washington apple with lemonade, basking in the sunlight of a beautiful fall day, he sat, basking in the musky air of a sick person's quarantine zone, swallowing extra-strength ibuprofen with water and eating saltine crackers. There he was, a twenty-year-old young man, finally out on his own, away from his parents, experiencing the freedom he'd dreamed of, and all he could think about was how much he wanted his mother.

After three days with a temperature reaching dangerous levels, his doctor recommended that if the temperature didn't break within another day, Jerrick should go to the hospital. Luckily, the temperature broke that night, and he finally stopped sweating. Knowing that Jerrick had a bit more energy, one of his friends came over and played some board games with him that night at the risk of getting sick himself. Even though the games wore him out, Jerrick was so grateful that his friend bravely entered the quarantine zone to provide Jerrick with some much-needed human interaction and fun. Looking back on the experience now, Jerrick remembers the compassion he felt from his friend coming over and spending time with him more than he remembers the fever. During Jerrick's negative, horrible experience with the swine flu, that friend taught Jerrick what being a true friend requires— selflessness, kindness, and some board games.

Like Jerrick, our teenagers can learn positive lessons from their negative experiences. As parents, we can help them along in this process by sharing how we've learned lessons from our own experiences, mistakes, or failed goals. Teenagers will learn how to find the positive lessons in their own lives by seeing how others have done the same.

Accept Responsibility

When mistakes are made or goals aren't accomplished, we can teach teenagers to accept responsibility for the choices that led to their mistakes or their unfulfilled goals rather than placing the blame on someone else.

A new eighth-grade teacher commented that some of her students had the mindset that "if they didn't pass the class, they think it's my fault. They think I failed them. In reality, they didn't do the work necessary for the grade they wanted. They didn't take advantage of the help I was willing to give them, and I had no choice but to fail them."

This mindset of placing the blame on someone else isn't true for all teenagers, but it happens more often than it should. We can teach teenagers the importance of accepting responsibility by doing the same ourselves.

During a family trip, Jerrick's dad was pulled over for speeding. The cop came to the passenger side window and asked Jerrick's dad, "Do you know why I pulled you over today?"

Jerrick's dad answered, "Yes, I was speeding." He didn't give any excuses, such as that the family was late for an appointment and needed to make up time or that the kids were cranky and he wanted to get to their destination quicker—both of which were true. His answer wasn't snide or snarky. He simply accepted responsibility for his actions, and in doing so, he set an example for his children.

Accepting responsibility for your actions is a bit like buying your own toy. A child will take better care of the toys he or she bought with his or her own money than of toys given by others. In a similar way, when teenagers accept responsibility for their actions, they take ownership of them and learn more from them than they would if we allow them to place the blame on someone else.

Maintain a Positive Attitude

We know a woman who had a goal to get married and start a family. Although she went on dates, met many wonderful men, and had great experiences, the stars haven't quite aligned, and she is still single with no family of her own. She's in her sixties now. She still would like to get married one day, but knows that, realistically, the odds are against her. Rather than becoming depressed or envious of others who have their own families, she maintains a positive attitude.

This woman treats her nieces and nephews as if they were her own children. She takes them on trips, attends their extracurricular activities, and shows genuine interest in their lives by listening to them, supporting them, and loving them. She hasn't let her unfulfilled goal suck the joy out of her life; instead, she serves others and maintains a positive attitude through those experiences.

Jerrick has a sister who is eighteen years old. She's gone through two knee surgeries, an ankle surgery, and a brain surgery—all in her high school years. She has recurring health problems that severely limit her quality of life. Rather than experiencing the joys of independence that a teenager feels by obtaining a driver's license, she's become dependent on a wheelchair to keep her mobile. Rather than putting down dates of homecoming dances or end-of-the-year parties on her calendar, she schedules doctors' visits and physical therapy sessions. Still, you'll never hear her complain. His sister has her bad days, certainly, but they are few and far between.

Jerrick's sister is able to maintain a positive attitude because of the support given to her by friends and family. Her younger sister and her niece cheer her up when she's having a rough day. When she's struggling to cope with pain, her friends come and keep her company. Her parents and siblings are always there supporting her and providing shoulders to lean on—physically and emotionally.

Jerrick remembers a time when he went back to his parents' house to visit for the holidays. His sister had just undergone double knee surgery and couldn't bend her legs. She was in a wheelchair and needed help to perform even the most basic tasks. One day, Jerrick and his dad took his sister into the bathroom so she could shower. The shower was a walk-in shower with enough room for his sister to sit down. Jerrick and his dad positioned the wheelchair next to the glass door leading into the shower and assumed their normal positions to lift his sister out of the wheelchair and into the shower—Jerrick's dad lifted his sister from under her armpits as Jerrick carefully lifted her legs to not bend her knees. Jerrick's dad walked backward into the shower, and as Jerrick followed, his dad accidentally hit the shower nob, turning on freezing cold water from the showerhead that headed straight for Jerrick's chest. It was a miracle that Jerrick didn't drop his sister's legs as the cold water chilled him to the bone!

After the water was turned off, everyone started laughing—Jerrick's sister included. The entire holiday break, his sister would laugh for no reason. When asked why she was laughing, she would reply, "Oh, I was just thinking about Jerrick's face when he got hit by the cold water." Jerrick's sister used that humorous experience to maintain a positive attitude for weeks.

Teenagers can learn to follow such examples. Teenagers can learn to find humor in life that can support them and allow them to maintain a positive attitude. Most importantly, we can provide support and encouragement to them as they fight to maintain a positive attitude. Our support—and the support of their friends and other family members—can sustain them.

Reassess Goals

When a goal isn't accomplished, teenagers must understand that doesn't mean it's all over. Often, a goal must be reevaluated, tweaked, and even changed to make it more doable.

Brad has never been a golfer; Jerrick, on the other hand, took golfing lessons in junior high school, and he has loved to golf ever since. Whenever he has a bad day on the golf course (which, unfortunately, is more often than not), he thinks of Kevin Na. The professional golfer from South Korea was having a pretty good day at the Valero Texas Open until one fateful hole—the par-4 number nine. In golf, a person shoots for the lowest score, which corresponds to the number of swings it takes to get the golf ball into the hole. This particular hole was supposed to take only four swings to finish, but Na took sixteen. He hit his first shot into the woods, and the rest was a nightmare. It was the worst score ever recorded on the Professional Golfers' Association of America (PGA) tour for a par 4 hole.

Na took the debacle in stride; he smiled and joked around after he finished the hole, and a year later he showed up at the same tournament and took a chainsaw to those woods that held him captive for so many shots. Na made some adjustments, reassessed his goals, and won his first PGA tournament just six months later.[2]

We can teach teenagers to follow Kevin Na's example and readjust their goals. Just because Na failed to reach his goal of winning the Valero Texas Open didn't mean that he failed in golf. He just needed to continue practicing and fine-tuning his skills. Eventually, that practice paid off. Just because teenagers may not accomplish their goals right now doesn't mean they won't accomplish them in the future.

Often, teenagers look on changing their goals as a sign of weakness. In reality, changing and readjusting goals is a sign of maturity. As we continually adjust and reassess our goals, our teenagers will learn that it's OK for them to do the same.

When a hedgehog rolls into a ball, sometimes you might get your finger caught in the quills from being overanxious to hug the hedgehog before he's calm enough to be picked up. You have to be patient and learn from your mistake. When teenagers stumble and are unable to achieve their goals, they can still learn important lessons and grow in times of unfulfillment. As parents, we can teach teenagers to accept responsibility, to maintain a positive attitude, and to reassess their goals now and then. The lessons and traits teenagers learn when they fail can help them as they strive for success.

Invitations to Action

How can you help teenagers when they don't accomplish their goals? Here are some notes that could change everything:

o What positive lessons have you learned from your failed goals? How can you teach your teenager the importance of looking for positive lessons?

o Do you hold your teenager responsible for their decisions? How does accountability relate to responsibility?

o What strategies do you use to help yourself maintain a positive attitude? Would those same strategies help your teenager? Who are positive role models you admire?

o How can you help your teenager avoid discouragement when goals have to be altered?

Endnotes:

1. Robert Burns and Allan Cunningham, *The Complete Works of Robert Burns: Containing His Poems, Songs, and Correspondence* (Charleston, SC: Nabu Press, 2010).

2. Jeff Shain, "Golfer Na Takes Revenge for 16 with a Chainsaw," *Chicago Tribune*, April 18, 2012.

Build Self-Esteem

How to Hug a Hedgehog Rule #3

"With both hands, scoop him up from the belly, which is covered with fur rather than quills. Let him explore you and become more comfortable with you."

A hedgehog becomes more comfortable as he gains confidence and begins to trust you. Teenagers also need to gain confidence—not just in others, but in themselves. They need to become more comfortable with others by being comfortable with themselves. Four helpful keys that we can teach our teens as they strive to develop healthy self-esteem are to recognize the difference between self-esteem and self-worth, to develop habits that will allow them to feel good about themselves, to act toward people and circumstances instead of reacting to them, and to find social acceptance by nurturing friendships.

Chapter 9

Recognize Self-Worth

"They're just beautiful," the wife said, almost out of habit, as she opened the carefully wrapped gift from her husband and took out a set diamond earrings to match her wedding band. Not recognizing their great value, she gave a half-hearted "Thank you."

Her husband, unaware of his wife's lack of interest in the gift, beamed to see his wife so pleased. She had once mentioned that someday she would like such a pair of earrings. He had saved a little each month for several years in order to buy them. The only problem was that his wife, thinking that there was no way in the world the husband could have afforded real diamonds, thought they were made from cubic zirconia, a synthesized material that looks like real diamond—but without the cost.

In the months that followed, she wore the earrings casually. She was careless when she put them on and took them off, and finally she misplaced one. When she told her husband, he became very concerned. Only then did she realize that the diamonds were real.

The worth of the stones had never changed. What had changed was how she esteemed the stones.

In the same way, it is essential for teenagers to realize that regardless of how they presently esteem themselves, they are of great worth. That fact never changes.

The many self-esteem seminars and school training programs available all miss the final mark if they do not lead participants past self-esteem to actual self-worth. One of the best ways to connect with teenagers is to help them realize their great worth.

External and Internal Sources of Self-Esteem

There are both external and internal sources of self-esteem. Externally, adults need to realize that self-esteem is not something we give someone so much as it is something we must stop taking away. Internally, teenagers must realize that their worth never changes, no matter how others treat them. Just as with the diamonds, as low as their self-esteem may plunge, their worth is still great.

True self-worth is the measure of our potential as human beings. It comes from within each of us individually as we come to know ourselves. Teenagers need to realize that they are unique and have worth to others and themselves. Their esteem will increase as they discover their worth.

One young woman we know struggled with self-esteem during her teen years. She told Brad, "So-and-so told me I'm too fat, and so-and-so told me I'm not fun to be with. I'm not as pretty or popular as my best friend. Not one boy has ever asked me out."

Brad asked, "Have you ever gone to the carnival fun house to look in the mirrors?"

"Yes," she said, "but what does that have to do with anything?"

He explained, "Those mirrors distort the truth. If we really believe the image of ourselves we see in those mirrors, it could cause some major problems. Can you imagine curling your hair or putting on makeup using one of those mirrors? It's the same way with self-esteem. Using the eyes of other people as our only mirrors will leave us with a distorted view."

Teenagers need to learn that what others think of them or say about them is one source of information, but it can't be their only source of information.

Author George D. Durrant said, "What someone else thinks about me is not the driving force for me that it once was."[1] That is the point that we must all reach: making self-esteem less external (relying on the input and influence of others) and more internal (relying on our own input and influence).

Brad used to teach sixth graders before he pursued other teaching opportunities at the university level. He knows that after parent-teacher conferences or open houses, people often approach teachers and say something kind. Casual onlookers might wonder if this praise is the source of self-esteem for these teachers. What those onlookers do not see or hear are the envious comments from other faculty members and hurtful letters that sometimes come from parents, criticizing even the most sincere efforts of teachers who are working in such a public arena. They don't hear the mean comments and cutting remarks of some students. For teachers whose only source of self-esteem is the input of others, such negative comments could lead to their resignations.

However, most teachers do what they do for internal reasons— to serve others and make a difference. This motivation brings balance. It doesn't matter how many people express compliments after an open house if the teacher does not feel pleased with his or her motives and work. On the other hand, some people may criticize a teacher and find fault, but it won't be the end of the world if the teacher is honestly pleased with his or her offerings. Like teachers, teenagers can feel their own worth regardless of how others choose to esteem them.

Recognizing Individual Worth

One excellent way to help teenagers realize their individual worth is to involve them in service. A youth leader once told Brad, "Young people with low self-esteem are in a downward cycle. Service is the cycle breaker. As they become busy serving and uplifting and healing others, they will not even notice that they are being helped themselves."

In her book *Lighten Up!*, Chieko Okazaki wrote, "We hear a lot about self-esteem these days. Self-esteem—the kind that really counts—comes from a personal relationship with others. Not a secondhand relationship of listening to someone else talk about us, but a personal relationship of talking, experiencing their love, and serving them."[2] As we cultivate in teenagers a healthy concern for others, we diminish the effects of their unhealthy concern for self.

Jerrick's mom moved from a small town in Idaho to Las Vegas, Nevada, during her teenage years. The high school she was zoned to attend had more students than her former town had residents, and the thought of that many peers intimidated her. She was concerned, like any person in new surroundings would be, about making friends and fitting in at her school. Instead of trying to make herself popular by trying out for sports, competing against others for being best-dressed, or even belittling others in an attempt to look cool, she chose to focus on building and uplifting others. She made a conscious effort every day to get to know people's names. When she would pass people in the hallway, she would greet them by name. It was her small way to show others she cared, and because she cared about others, she focused less on herself. Consequently, people in the hallway and in class could tell that Jerrick's mom really cared about them, and they wanted to be her friends.

Jerrick remembers when he decided to run for a student body office at his school. While offering advice and encouragement, his mom would say, "Just greet people in the hallways by name and really show an interest in them. They'll vote for you when they know you're rooting for them." The philosophy worked for Jerrick as it had for his mom. As his relationships with his fellow classmates grew, his own confidence grew as well. He focused less on his perceived imperfections as he focused more on his relationship with others.

Brad had a difficult time in junior high school. A boy who has no basket-shooting skills often suffers in elementary school and agonizes in junior high. The students in his junior high came from several different elementary schools, and many who suffered from insecurity picked on others.

Somehow, in the shuffle, Brad ended up at the bottom of the pecking order. Each day, he had to face the threats, rejection, and hurtful criticisms of classmates. Once he was in that position, it seemed as if nothing he did was right. If he tried to talk and be friendly, he was mocked. If he didn't, others made fun of him anyway. He hated the pain and the hurt, but—and this is the point—through it all, he did not hate himself.

Brad always had the feeling that they just didn't know him. Because of the praise, acceptance, and encouragement he'd received from parents and cousins, he liked himself. Because he knew he was valuable, he valued himself. The fact that the kids at his new school didn't like him did not seem like evidence to him that he was a bad person. Rather, it was simply evidence that they did not know him.

As Brad and his classmates grew and matured, they came to know each other better. He reached out in service, and his efforts brought acceptance. Brad's self-esteem was tested, but because of the knowledge he had of his true self-worth, he was able to weather the storm. Because he cared more about being a friend to others than simply finding friends for himself, he focused outward and found acceptance.

Who Teenagers Really Are

The greatest thing we can do to help young people improve self-esteem is to help them come to know who they really are. Through this, they will come to know of their self-worth, and when they know their true worth, their self-esteem will increase.

As a friend of ours concluded teaching a seminar on self-esteem, a man walked up to the front of the room and asked, "May I say something?" This friend handed the microphone to him, and he told the following story:

> When I was eight years old, I was really into baseball. I had every player's baseball card. My dad saved his money to send me to a baseball camp run by a star player.
>
> The first day, the famous man running the camp—a man who was kind of cocky—pulled out a list of names and asked, "Where's Step-han?" My name is spelled

with a *ph* instead of a *v*. He purposefully mispronounced it.

I cringed as everyone started to laugh.

The coach continued to call, "Step-han, are you here? Hey, Step-han."

I felt worse and worse. Everyone was laughing. It was the worst experience of my life to that point. When I got home, I told my dad I would never play baseball again.

My dad was a wise man and waited a few years. Then, a retired player came to town and started a Little League program. Dad took the new coach aside and said, "My son loves baseball very much, but he had a bad experience with a coach." And he told the new coach the whole story.

The new coach said, "You send him to me for tryouts."

I barely made the team, but I improved as the season progressed. Then the time came when it was a win-or-lose situation for my team. The bases were loaded, and it was my turn at bat. I thought the coach was going to send in a pinch hitter for me, but he didn't. He walked over and put his arm around me and said, "Stephen, you can do it. I'm your coach, and I'm behind you all the way. You can do it."

I walked up to the plate, and the pitcher threw the ball. I did not hit it out of the ballpark, but I did hit a fly to the center fielder that was deep enough to allow the runner from third to beat the throw to home. Our team won the game.

We must help teens overlook the denigrating voices of those around them and listen to the voice within themselves—the voice telling them, "You can do this! You know you can." In those moments, they glimpse who they really are, and someone with that vision is never the same again.

The pilot light on Jerrick's gas stove at home recently broke. In order to turn on his stove, he had to use a lighter to ignite the gas and start the flame. Teenagers are like the stove. That voice inside teenagers—the voice telling them they can do it—can occasionally go out because of the degrading voices that surround them. When that happens, we must become their lighters and give them positive encouragement until they once again hear that voice within themselves.

How do you know if you're on the way to gaining the trust of your hedgehog? Sometimes, even after you pick up your hedgehog, he might still roll into a ball. The key in that situation is not to panic! After a few minutes, the hedgehog will unroll and begin exploring, and then you'll know you are on the way to a trusting relationship. How do parents know if teenagers are gaining trust in themselves? If teenagers begin to serve and cultivate a healthy concern for others, if they begin to diminish the effects of negative feelings for self, and if they find self-acceptance as they start to understand their own unique self-worth, we know teenagers are well on their way to a healthy knowledge of who they really are. With hedgehogs and with teens, our patient efforts are worthwhile. Our teenagers can come to recognize their great worth and potential.

Invitations to Action

How can you help your teenager recognize his or her own self-worth? Here are some thoughts to keep in mind:

○ What were some reasons why you might have had low self-esteem as a teenager? How can sharing your experiences help your teenager?

○ How can you and your teenager engage in meaningful service to others?

○ Think of a time when you recognized the great worth of your teenager. Tell your teenager about that experience. How can you continue to look for and express belief in the potential of your teenager?

Endnotes:

1. George D. Durrant, *My Best Day So Far*, (Salt Lake City: Bookcraft, 1990).
2. Chieko Okazaki, *Lighten Up!* (Salt Lake City: Deseret Book, 1993).

Chapter 10

Help Teens Develop a Positive Self-Image

Toward the end of eighth grade, Jerrick's junior high science club entered a statewide competition. He and two other friends were chosen to represent their school. They were to give a presentation on their ideas for creating a more environmentally friendly city infrastructure and take part in a question-and-answer session afterwards. Although it was scary being in front of so many people and not knowing what questions were going to be asked, Jerrick and his friends did well. Their school did the best they had ever done in the competition that year, which helped the presenters feel especially good about their work.

When Jerrick and his friends entered high school a few months later, they discovered that the popular kids didn't spend time in science classrooms after school. Each one of the presenters still enjoyed science, but because of peer pressure, they all chose to follow different paths in high school. Although they had high self-esteem at the end of junior high, they all grappled with low self-esteem for a time during their adjustment into high school.

One of the teenager's struggle with low self-esteem was very difficult. Because she was so smart, she started to be the target of bullying from other students. They also teased her because of her weight. Slowly, she let the perceptions of others begin to affect her image of herself. She started hanging out with a different crowd, using drugs and alcohol, and skipping class. Eventually, she was transferred to a different high school because she kept getting into trouble. Sadly, this bright young woman hasn't been able to live up to her potential. She was closer to it in junior high than she is today.

In order for teenagers to have high self-esteem, they need to develop a positive self-image. That doesn't mean they need to—nor should they—conform to the media's standard of perfection, but they need to be comfortable with themselves. As we help them understand the difference between the real and the ideal, take care of their physical well-being, stop the unhealthy habit of comparison, and adopt healthy habits in its place, teenagers can begin to reap the benefits of high self-esteem.

The Real Versus the Ideal

One of our favorite pastimes is watching wholesome movies with our families. While watching movies, audience members are asked to suspend reality for a time and enter the magical world of the movie. Nowhere is this more evident than Disney and Pixar's popular *Toy Story* series.

In *Toy Story*, Andy's toys come to life whenever he or other humans aren't around. The toys have many adventures and develop new friendships as they help each other overcome their problems. Of course, we know that toys don't actually come to life, but younger children often maintain that belief. Jerrick's youngest sister did, and Jerrick even admits that he used to pretend his toy knights could talk. Brad used to have puppets that seemed like real people in his young mind.

Children grow up and begin to recognize and distinguish between fiction and fact, unreal and real. However, teenagers often have difficulty distinguishing between the real and the ideal—the realities of life versus the ideals that are constantly placed before them by magazines, movies, the Internet, and the media. As parents, we may play along with and encourage childish beliefs, but we must help teens distinguish between the real and the ideal.

One parent we know describes the real versus the ideal this way: "While watching a movie, we only see one part of the equation. When you try and think in 360 degrees, you discover all that goes into the movie: all the sets, the cameras, the directors; all the outtakes, the makeup, and the stunt people. Teenagers need to think in that same way when it comes to their lives. They need to look at the perfect picture of a beautiful model on the Internet and see the entire picture: the hairdressers, the makeup artists, and the Photoshop experts. Then teenagers will see the reality of the ideal (and unrealistic) image."

As we help teenagers realize that they only see part of the picture when it comes to the ideals put before them, teenagers will understand that it's unhealthy and dangerous to expect to conform themselves to the media's fictional world. Children mature when they realize that their toys don't have lives of their own. Teenagers' self-esteem will also mature as they realize that it's OK to be real and not conform to an impossible ideal.

Physical Well-Being

On one particularly chilly March night, Jerrick and his college roommate, Chris, decided to go shoot some hoops at a lighted outdoor basketball court near their apartment. They had both just finished an extremely busy week and desperately needed to unwind. An intense game of one-on-one seemed like the perfect remedy for such a situation.

One sore back, a fat lip, and a couple hours later, they decided to call it a night (much to the dismay of Jerrick, who desperately wanted to redeem himself after being beaten by Chris more than a few times). They walked home, joking around and having a fun time trying to talk with numb mouths from the cold.

After taking a long, hot shower, Jerrick was still shivering. "I think I may be getting a cold," he told Chris. "I'm going to head to bed early."

"Oh, please," Chris joked back, "you know you're just feeling bad from getting beaten so many times out on the court."

Jerrick played along, "Yeah, that's it. I'm sure I'll feel better tomorrow morning once I forget about tonight." He desperately hoped he'd feel better that next morning, but he had a feeling things weren't about to get better anytime soon.

That next morning, Jerrick woke up with a fever and intense back pain. He took some medication and tried to sleep it off, but the pain just kept getting worse. Soon, it was accompanied with nausea and dehydration. He went to the doctor's office and discovered, much to his dismay, that he had contracted the family curse: kidney stones.

For the next few days, Jerrick spent most of his time curled up in a ball on his couch, save for a day in the urgent care hooked up to an IV. Eventually, the kidney stones passed (ouch!), and he was finally able to get back to regular life.

During a follow-up appointment, Jerrick's doctor wanted to examine his lifestyle and try and decrease the risk of him developing any more stones.

"Do you smoke or drink alcoholic beverages?" Jerrick's doctor asked.

"No," He replied.

"Are you getting enough water?"

"I think so."

"Do you drink soda or coffee?"

"Well, I drink a couple cans of soda a day. It helps me stay awake," Jerrick replied.

His doctor told him that studies have shown consuming one soda a day increases the risk of kidney stones. Jerrick quit drinking caffeinated sodas from that day on, and for good measure, started drinking more water each day. "I'd do anything to avoid getting kidney stones again," he said.

Even though Jerrick thought he was relatively healthy—he exercised regularly, got plenty of sleep, and ate balanced meals—those sodas contributed to pain that he wished he didn't ever feel. He expected to see physical benefits from drinking less soda, and he did. What he didn't expect, however, was the emotional and mental benefits that he has experienced as a direct result of his diet change. He has better control over his temper, better focus, and better energy since he stopped drinking soda. Any positive health changes can bring about those other types of benefits. Teenagers need to understand that not only will eating right and taking care of their bodies increase their overall physical health but also that their efforts will have emotional and mental health benefits. It will affect how they feel about themselves.

Comparison

One young man we know was homeschooled for much of his elementary school years and had little contact with other children beyond his own siblings. Because of changing family circumstances, this young man entered public school during his seventh grade year. One can imagine the shock this boy, fresh from a loving environment with little negativity, experienced as he learned about the ins and outs of junior high school.

One day, this boy came home and sadly declared, "I'm a nobody!"

"Why do you say that?" his mother inquired.

"Some kids at school laughed at my clothes and told me I don't fit in. They said I'm a nobody, and I am. I wear hand-me-downs, Mom. No one will want to hang out with *this*," he said, gesturing to himself. The young man's new surroundings and new peers had influenced him in a negative way.

Sadly, many teenagers feel the same way because they compare themselves to their peers. They say, "My clothes aren't as new as his," "I'm not as good at sports as she is," or "His cell phone is cooler than mine." While some amount of comparison is normal and can help teenagers push themselves to be better, an unhealthy amount of comparison is toxic to self-esteem. Teenagers with the worst images of themselves often spend the most time comparing themselves to others on social media and in real life. We can help teenagers focus on finding the good in themselves. As they do this, teenagers will learn that one opinion matters most: their own.

Appearance

Even though we continually try to teach teenagers that what's inside is what really counts, we can't change the fact that teenagers base much of their self-esteem on how they look. Teenagers agonize over their complexions and their weight during an awkward stage of their lives, a stage filled with acne, uncoordinated limbs, braces, and growth spurts. They focus more on their self-perceived lists of defects rather than the things they like about themselves.

In the old movie *What About Bob?*, the character Bob Wiley keeps repeating the line, "I feel good. I feel great. I feel wonderful."[1] It is his attempt to affect the way he feels about the situation he is in, which most people would say isn't good, great, or wonderful. In a similar way, teens can often affect the way they think about a situation by telling themselves, "I feel good. I feel great. I feel wonderful." However, it gets harder when they try to tell themselves "I look good. I look great. I look wonderful." In order to help teenagers feel good about the way they look, we need to honestly compliment something good about them. It will do wonders for their self-esteem. We all have things we secretly like about ourselves, as well as things we don't. When parents and family members validate the good, it can offset those who accentuate the bad.

Jerrick remembers a time when he went to a wedding of an extended family member he hadn't seen in many months. He knew a few of his younger teenage cousins in particular were having a hard time with schoolwork and making friends, so he tried to pay extra attention to them and spend some time with them. When he saw one of them first walk through the door, he walked up to him and noticed what a nice tie his cousin had on. The knot on the tie even had a perfectly placed dimple. It was obvious the young man had spent some time getting it just right. Jerrick said, "I like your tie! You made a great choice. It looks awesome!" The smile and subsequent "Thank you" from his cousin let Jerrick know that his compliment hadn't been blown off.

After the hedgehog starts exploring, you can carefully grab a treat with one hand and offer it to your hedgehog. By offering treats occasionally while you handle your hedgehog, you will help the hedgehog learn to enjoy being held. As teenagers explore the changing world around them, we can help them feel better about themselves. We can remind teens to distinguish the real from the ideal, to gain better physical well-being, to stop comparing themselves to others. Just like you extend treats to a hedgehog, you can sincerely compliment teens on their appearance and achievements, and they will begin to develop a positive self-image.

Invitations to Action

How can you help teenagers feel better about themselves? Here are keys that, when practiced, will make a difference:

- How do you differentiate between your own expectations and the expectations of others? What are your expectations for your teenager? How can you adjust your expectations to be more positive and/or reasonable?

- How do you promote your teenager's physical well-being? What other ways can you promote it without mandating it? What kind of example are you setting?

- Think of a time when you have compared yourself to others. What did you learn? How can you share what you learned through that experience with your teenager?

- How do you feel about your teenager's appearance? What sincere compliments can you offer? How can you compliment them more consistently?

Endnotes:

1. *What About Bob?* Touchstone Pictures, 1991.

Chapter 11

Act! Don't React

As a young man, Brad attended a dance in Mexico when he was there on a school trip. The weather was perfect, and the mood was just right for an awkward young man to take a swipe at love. This is his story of what happened that night:

"Alright, all you boys, there are lots of girls who would love to dance this next slow song, so let's get busy." Our tour adviser looked directly at Jason and me and then turned on the music again. A tropical breeze shuffled through leaves in a planter behind us on the hotel patio.

I had just finished the eighth grade and didn't even know how to dance myself, let alone ask a girl to do it with me.

"I guess we should go dance, Brad." Jason was rolling up the embroidered sleeves of the "I'm-a-tourist-in-Mexico" shirt he had bought that afternoon.

"No, not me."

"But Mr. J said there are girls who want to dance, and anyway this is the last night of the trip and we'll probably never see them again." A sudden gust blew Jason's hair across his eyes. Casually, he pushed it back again.

This educational tour through Mexico had been sponsored by our school district, and up to now it had been a great experience. Why did they have to spoil it with a dance?

"Come on." Jason pulled me up. "You ask Joan, and I'll ask Christie." He buttoned his top shirt button, moved across the patio, and offered his hand. "Hey, Christie, would you like to dance?"

I stood back and watched in hopes of learning instantly the intricacies of social interaction.

Christie flipped her hair. "Gee, uh, thanks, Jason, but not right now."

"What about you, Joan?" he asked.

From my safe position behind the lines, I noticed Jason's crooked-tooth smile. I saw my friend for the first time as those girls might be seeing him, and I guess overall he did look kind of unusual.

"I'd really like to dance, Jason, but I don't like this song," Joan answered.

He tugged at his gaudy new shirt. "Well, maybe later?"

The two embarrassed girls looked quickly at each other. "Oh, uh . . . we're not feeling too well."

After a moment, Jason came back to me. "OK, Brad, who should we ask next?"

I still couldn't believe what Joan had said. "Not feeling well! She felt good enough to dance with Monroe a few minutes ago," I complained to Jason.

"But he's a senior in high school. We're only eighth graders."

"Ninth graders now," I reminded. I followed him to the tile fountain in the center of the patio, where Stephanie stood. With her hand on her hip and her nose in the air, she might as well have been a water-spouting statue.

I realized what Jason was about to do even before he said, "Hey, Stephanie, how about a dance?"

"Jason, don't . . . " I turned away with elaborate casualness. Stephanie broke her pose to smile disdainfully and glide haughtily away.

"Well, how about it? You want to dance?" Jason called after her.

She didn't even bother to look back.

With my finger, I poked a ripple into the fountain pool. "I don't get it, Jas. I thought girls liked to dance."

"They do," he assured me. "Look, why don't you ask Stephanie?"

"No way! Not her. I don't want to get turned down, too."

With his fingers, Jason jarred the water like I did, again contorting our shadowed reflections. "Brad, if Stephanie doesn't want to dance, it's her problem, not yours."

"But if she said no to you, why should I ask her?"

"Why not?"

The director turned up the music again. Jason stepped closer to me to be heard. "Why should you let her decide how you're going to act?" He pushed his fingers through his hair again. "I'm going over there to ask some new girls. Want to come?"

I shook my head and sat on the tile rim of the fountain. It felt cold in the evening. Jason walked away, stepping awkwardly to the beat.

As I think back on that incident, I realize that Jason acted toward people. Most of us react to them. Jason knew what he wanted and how he should behave. If Stephanie had refused me like that, I'd have either crawled off and buried myself in a Mexican pyramid or said, "You're not so neat yourself," and maybe bitten her ankle or something.

I remember myself that evening as though I were a character in a cartoon, sitting by that cold fountain thinking, but with nothing written in my thought bubble. If I were to fill it in now, I guess I'd write, *No one is more miserable than the dummy who always reacts.*

At that long-ago dance, my center of confidence was outside myself, being kicked around that patio like an old can. If Christie had said, "You're cold," I'd have shivered. If Monroe had said, "You're hot," I'd have sweated. My feelings toward the whole situation were totally dependent upon a few people who could decide if I would be embarrassed or proud, rude or gracious, introverted or extroverted. Unlike Jason, whose emotional security was rooted within himself, I had relinquished control of my own personality. I might as well have been a puppet allowing anyone who passed by to pull my strings.

I'm thankful for my skinny, unkempt eighth-grade friend and for the important principle he personified—to act and not react—for in all the dances I've attended since then, not once have I bitten any girl's ankle.

Establish a Pattern of Acting

Perhaps one of the most important characteristics we can demonstrate and encourage as we connect with teens is acting toward people and situations rather than reacting to them. It is easy to fall into a pattern of reacting: "I'm not saying hi to him. He didn't say hi to me." "I'm not inviting her to my party. She never invited me to hers." "I'm not writing him another email until he answers the one I already sent. It's his turn." Teens can understand that it takes a great deal of character and personal courage to cut those puppet strings and stop letting other people have that much power in our lives.

We need to help teenagers establish positive patterns of acting instead of reacting: "I am going to say hi whether he waves back or not." "If I have a rotten day, I allowed it. If I have a great day, I'm the one who helped make that happen." "Others don't have to change so I can feel better."

Obviously, our society admires actors. We see their images all around us, and they become idols for many. However, that's not the kind of acting we're talking about. It's easy to be confident and stand up to the bad guys when the script is written out in advance and the happy ending is guaranteed. It's easy to act self-assured when there is a stunt man ready to step in the minute the going gets rough.

The "actors" we admire most are not on stage or in film. Rather, they are ordinary people who face situations and challenges not of their choosing and yet refuse to let circumstances pull their strings. Think of the person in a wheelchair who stays upbeat and positive, even when someone without a sticker has parked in the handicapped space. Think about the kid whose parents went through an ugly divorce, yet he continues to love them both. Think of the girl who was not selected the winner of a scholarship, but who refuses to let herself become bitter or angry about it. These are the ones who win "best actor" and "best actress" awards from us by refusing to react.

A man we'll call Kurt is a great example of refusing to react to circumstances. Before he married his sweetheart, he dated lots of different girls. Kurt loved to be thoughtful and was always thinking of little things that he could do to show his interest in a girl like giving her chocolate-covered strawberries or sending her notes of encouragement before a big job interview. The girls that were interested in Kurt appreciated the gestures, but the girls that weren't interested did not. Some were even rude to Kurt because of the gestures. After one particularly not-so-nice encounter, Jerrick asked Kurt, "Why do you keep doing things for girls? You just end up getting hurt."

Kurt replied, "I like doing those things, and no one is going to make me stop doing something good."

True to his word, Kurt acted and refused to let his circumstances get the better of him. His wife now loves the little things he does for her to show his love.

Our lives are full of daily dramas, and each of us plays a part in schools, families, and communities. Our applause goes to the girl who welcomes the newcomer and the guy who picks up litter, even when it's not for a service project or class assignment. We cheer for the athlete who can be treated unfairly by the coach and still push himself to do his best; the driver on the freeway who gets sworn at or flipped off and doesn't return fire. These are the "actors" who get our standing ovations.

Emulating Positive Examples

A university put together a youth retreat on the East Coast at which young people had gathered from several different states to get to know each other.

A girl named Teri had braces on her legs and two canes she used as she struggled to walk from place to place. There were many different workshops throughout the day that the teens could chose to attend, and Teri had to walk a considerable distance to get to where one teacher was presenting. It meant a lot to the teacher that she would make that extra-mile sacrifice.

After the workshop concluded, the teacher wanted to thank Teri for coming, but several of the other young people surrounded him quickly. The teacher tried his best to listen and respond, but he kept glancing from time to time at Teri, who was moving slowly toward the door. He didn't want to be rude to the young people around him, but he also knew he needed to acknowledge Teri before his chance was gone.

Finally, the teacher simply interrupted the youth by his side and called out across the room, "Teri, thanks for coming. I'll see you tonight at the dance. Save me a dance."

The whole room became silent. The young people near the teacher just stared incredulously. Teri turned completely around and, after a pause that seemed to last for an hour, said, "I don't dance."

The teacher felt stupid. He wished he could vacuum up the words he had just uttered and start over.

Teri forced a smile, turned, and left. The teacher wanted to crawl away and hide. He loved teenagers and would never purposely do anything to hurt a young person, and obviously Teri had been hurt and embarrassed by what he said. He felt sick.

That evening, the teacher knew he needed to attend the dance as a chaperone, but he was hardly in the mood anymore. Still, he made his way into the gym, where he found all the youth standing around the sides. Music was playing. Lights were dimmed. The dance should have started by now, yet everyone was just standing around waiting for someone else to start dancing.

The teacher thought, *Why aren't these young people acting instead or reacting?* Suddenly, he heard someone yell his name. The teacher turned to see Teri standing in the middle of the dance floor in a pretty dress, waving him over with one of her canes.

"Get over here and dance with me," she called out.

All eyes turned to where the teacher was standing. *Me?* The teacher thought. *You want* me *to go out there and start this dance? But I'm old. What will everyone think?* Then, almost at the same moment, he thought of Teri. A girl who could hardly walk had the courage to start this dance, and he was worried about what people would think of him. He felt foolish. Here was a young woman who found the courage to act and not react, and he was worried about himself.

That was a personal turning point in the teacher's life. Sure, he was willing to teach teenagers, but was he willing to learn from them? Was he willing to act and not react? Was he willing to cut the puppet strings once and for all? The teacher smiled, walked confidently out to the dance floor, hugged Teri, and then had a blast dancing with this incredible young woman.

When picking up your hedgehog, you will need to act. If you were to just put your hands out expecting the hedgehog to walk onto them, the hedgehog might never make his way onto your hands. Instead, you must actively put both hands under the hedgehog and scoop him up. In a similar way, teenagers need to act and not react. We connect with teens by demonstrating patterns of acting for teenagers and then helping them establish similar patterns of acting and not reacting. In this way, they can not only learn to enjoy school dances, but the dance that really matters—the one we call life.

Invitations to Action

How can you help your teenager learn to act and not react to the people and circumstances in his or her life? Here are a few keys to consider:

- How do you respond in certain situations? Are you acting or reacting toward them? What will you do to better establish a pattern of acting that your teenager can emulate?

- Think of someone you admire. How has his or her example affected you? Can you think of people in your teenager's life who are positive examples of acting and not reacting?

Chapter 12

T-H-I-N-K Friendship

Many elementary schools have a tradition of holding "field days" on which different activities are held in a style similar to the Olympics. Medals are given based on how well students perform in different activities. Jerrick remembers when he was in third grade and he was excited to participate in field day with the fourth and fifth-graders. He woke up that morning ready to go have some fun, make friends with the fifth-graders, and maybe even earn some medals. While waiting in line for one of the activities, some of the older boys behind him began making fun of his ears. "Look at those ears! He looks like Dumbo," one said.

Another chimed in, laughing, "Do you think he can fly? That's not fair. He shouldn't be allowed to compete in the games."

Those field day activities suddenly weren't as fun for Jerrick. He came home, visibly troubled, and his mom asked, "Are you OK?"

"Some of the fifth-graders made fun of me today," Jerrick responded. "They said I have big ears and called me 'Dumbo.'"

"You do not have big ears. Don't listen to those bullies. They're just trying to make themselves feel better by putting you down," his mom tried to reassure him.

Jerrick recalls, "I remember getting really angry at my mom for saying that I don't have big ears. I rather emphatically told her, 'You're lying! The kids at school said I have big ears, so you're lying!' I valued my classmates' opinions over my own mother's."

Even as a child, classmates' opinions were important to Jerrick. Children naturally wish to be valued and appreciated by their peers, and this longing magnifies during teenage years. Teenagers are acutely aware of the opinions of others, especially their friends, which partly explains why teenagers desire and value friendship above almost anything else.

In a large study of teenagers, 76 percent reported that having friends was of great importance to them.[1] However, what teenagers really crave is the feeling that having friends brings to them— the feeling of social acceptance, which greatly influences teenagers' self-esteem. Social acceptance is a sense of belonging that is influenced by what others think and say about teenagers. In addition to friends, teenagers are also influenced by the messages communicated by parents, teachers, relatives, and other adults.

Social acceptance seems pretty straightforward until you realize that what people are actually saying or thinking does not really affect self-esteem so much as what a teenager *perceives* is being said and thought, just like how Jerrick's perception of the fifth-graders influenced his own self-esteem. However, teenagers' perceptions of themselves don't have to be negative. In fact, a recent study suggests that "teens' perceptions of their own social success may be a crucial predictor of long-term social functioning, such that even teens who are not broadly popular may demonstrate positive adjustment over time if they maintain a positive internal sense of their social acceptance."[2] In other words, the way teenagers view their own social acceptance will affect their self-esteem—either positively or negatively.

We're not suggesting that parents do whatever it takes to help their teens be popular with the "in" crowd. Instead, we, as parents, must help teens realize that they should and will be valued for who they are by the people who count. Based on our experience, a healthy self-esteem, bolstered by the influence of good friends and a positive view of social acceptance, can help teens become more empathetic, selfless, and accepting of other viewpoints. So how can we help teenagers have a positive view of their own social acceptance? We can teach teens to **T-H-I-N-K** about friendships by **trying** new things, **helping** others, **investing** in themselves, **nurturing** positive emotions, and **keeping** a healthy perspective.

Trying New Things

Because of that comment back in third grade, Jerrick tried to hide his ears all throughout middle school and most of high school. He never wore hats because he thought they made his ears stick out more than they already did. He even grew his hair out so the hair would cover his ears. Looking back on pictures of that hair now, Jerrick regrets that decision.

Midway through middle school, things began to change. Jerrick loved basketball, even though he wasn't very good at it. He played basketball in a youth league up until about seventh grade. That year, he decided to focus more on science club instead of basketball. He just didn't feel like he belonged on his basketball teams, and he wasn't as dedicated to the sport as others around him seemed to be. His idea of his own social acceptance began to sink, and with it, his self-esteem. Even though science club helped his self-esteem start to rise, his mom could see that he needed a new sport. She convinced him to try playing volleyball instead. Jerrick found security in volleyball because his hard work in that sport made him feel good about himself. The comments about his ears never changed, but gradually, he began to perceive those comments in a different way. About halfway through high school, when his classmates or players from the team he was playing against on a given night would comment that he had Dumbo ears, he perceived it as a compliment. *That's right! These ears help me jump higher and make me fly*, he would think.

If teenagers are having a difficult time feeling socially accepted, trying new things can help. Jerrick discovered a talent of his that he didn't know existed by trying new things, and he found friends through volleyball with whom he still remains close today. None of it would have been possible without the support and encouragement of his family, especially his mom. Whatever positive new things our teenagers try, it is important for us to support them in their endeavors. Teenagers need to feel socially accepted within their family, too, and we can help them feel socially accepted by supporting them as they try new things.

Helping Others

During Brad's early childhood years, he lived in Ethiopia, Africa. When he was eight, his family moved back to the United States, and Brad faced many difficult adjustments. In Ethiopia, American sports weren't emphasized, and Brad didn't grow up playing any sort of ball— baseball, football, volleyball, or basketball.

When he moved back to the United States, he found himself feeling left out at recess. Whenever the class would pick teams for basketball, he was always chosen last. Sometimes he jokingly brags that when he was in elementary school, the team captains would usually fight over him. What he doesn't say is that the fight was over which team was going to get stuck with him. Pretty soon, he simply stopped trying to play altogether and turned his attention to other interests.

In junior high, the P.E. class most boys looked forward to was the one Brad dreaded. One day, the regular coach wasn't there, and the class was covered by a substitute who divided the group into relay teams. The substitute explained that each team member would be expected to run to the other side of the gym, climb the rope, and run back. The first team finished would win. Eagerly, the boys lined up. Brad made his way slowly to the back of his line. His regular coach knew he couldn't climb the rope. Brad knew he couldn't climb the rope. The top of the rope might as well have been the top of Mount Everest.

"Ready, set, go!" The substitute coach blew his whistle, and the race began. In the heat of competition, the boys yelled wildly for their teammates. Helplessly, Brad awaited his turn—his heart thumping in fear. As he got closer to the front of the line, he worked out a plan in his mind: he would run as fast as he could, grab the rope, and pull himself up until the coach wasn't looking. Then he could slide down and run back to his place. He didn't want his teammates losing the race because of him.

When Brad's turn in the relay came, he ran to the rope and pulled with all his strength. He could hardly lift himself above the ground. His arms shook as he struggled just to hold on. When he glanced toward the coach and found he wasn't watching, Brad let go of the rope. He dropped to the ground and was running back to his place when suddenly, to his horror, the coach blew his whistle and started yelling. Everyone stopped and the gym grew silent.

The coach pointed at Brad and yelled, "Alright, young man. We will have no cheating in this race! Get back to that rope and climb it all the way to the top." In humiliation, Brad returned to the rope as the entire class gathered to watch. Amid the smirks and laughter of his peers, he began struggling unsuccessfully to climb the rope until, at last, he was rescued by the shower bell.

That was a horrible experience for Brad. Even now, it's an embarrassing and painful memory for him. Brad says, "I guess I could have become angry. I could have quit school, ditched the class, or taken my frustration out by yelling at the coach or other students. I could have become depressed and withdrawn. Instead, I made a vow to myself that I would never treat anyone else like that. I determined to always try to treat others with more respect, empathy, and kindness than I was shown on that occasion."

In the years that followed, Brad tried to notice when others were suffering. In his school, there was a shy, awkward boy with a birth defect that had left his face somewhat deformed. Brad went out of his way to find the boy in the hall and sit by him in classes. The young man worked in the lunchroom scraping trays. Brad signed up to work there, too, so the young man wouldn't be alone.

On another occasion, Brad overheard a group of girls gossiping about another girl. One girl asked, "Did you hear the news about Jenny? She's moving!"

Another girl flipped her hair and said, "I'm glad, because I can't stand her."

Yet another joined in, saying, "She bugs me, too! She thinks she's so cool, and she's not! I'm glad we won't have to put up with her anymore."

Brad decided that Jenny didn't need people talking about her as much as she might need friends. He gathered some of his classmates and put together a surprise going-away party to wish Jenny well in her new school.

Brad began to lose himself in quiet, sincere service to others, and, ironically, he began to find himself. The more he worried about others, the less he worried about himself and the more he began to be accepted by his peers. By the time he graduated from high school, he had been blessed with many friends.

What had caused such a change? Did Brad buy a super car? No, he drove an old heap of a Chevy. Had he become a super athlete? No, he still couldn't climb a rope. Had he worked out and become slim and strong? No, he just tried to be nice. He made a conscious effort to defend the underdog and compliment others when they did something well. He didn't link himself to this group or that group; he attempted to be friendly to everyone.

When the night of his senior dinner dance came, Brad certainly never dreamed he would receive any recognition. He knew he wouldn't be named "Most Likely to Succeed" or get the award for being the smartest, coolest, or best-looking. In fact, when the senior class officers called out his name and asked him to come to the front, he couldn't imagine why. He hoped they weren't going to ask him to climb a rope! They didn't. Instead, they presented him with an award that meant much more to him than they will ever know. They named Brad the "Most-Loved Senior." His classmates actually stood and applauded. Imagine—a standing ovation from some of the very young people who had teased and ridiculed Brad in junior high.

One of the most effective ways to encourage social acceptance in teenagers is to teach them to help others. As they help others, their perception of the way people feel about them will grow. They may find, like Brad did, that they've developed lasting friendships along the way.

Investing in Themselves

A large part of teenagers' views on social acceptance centers on accepting themselves. When teenagers feel good about themselves, it's easier for them to perceive the words and actions of others as positive words and actions, thereby finding social acceptance among their peers and adults. As with trying new things and helping others, social acceptance can improve as teens are encouraged to invest in developing their talents.

Each teenager is different. Each teenager has different abilities, and trying new things will help them discover those talents, but discovering them isn't enough. One of the new activities Jerrick tried in high school to boost his social acceptance was singing. He joined his high school's choir originally because some of his friends were in it, but he soon discovered that he liked to sing and wanted to get better at it and improve his vocal range.

He started singing more and more—in high school, in church choirs, in the car, and, of course, in the shower. His senior year, Jerrick decided to try out for the most prestigious choir at his high school. He practiced constantly, went to the auditions, and much to his surprise, he made it! In fact, by the middle of his senior year, he was in four different choirs at his high school all because he practiced and invested some time in self-development.

The dedication he invested into singing also led to more opportunities. His choir director noticed Jerrick's dedication and decided to make him a section leader in the concert choir at the high school. Having the choir director notice him was a bonus, but Jerrick's self-esteem already improved because of the effort he put into something he loved.

As teenagers invest some time and effort in developing talents, they will find their perception of their social acceptance will grow.

Like Jerrick's choir director, we can help teenagers by noticing their efforts and opening doors of opportunity.

Nurturing Positive Emotions

A young woman once told Brad, "I feel so inadequate, so inferior, so average. I watch and study everyone around me—people, pictures in magazines, actresses, everyone—picking out every feature that I wish I could have for myself. In every person, I see a trait that I rip myself apart for not having or for not being able to do as well. Envy has made me a depressed and hopeless person. I am overweight. My hair's a mess. My eyebrows are each different. My eyelashes grow every direction. My nose is long—even my mother would admit this, because she has the same one, only not quite as bad."

Unfortunately, more and more teenagers face this type of self-deprecation because it's relatively easy to compare themselves to others in the digital age. All they need to do is look at the number of their Facebook friends or the number of retweets on Twitter. They see the "perfect" lives of others presented on social media and feel shortchanged. When teenagers are faced with this decreasing view of their own social acceptance, they can become negative toward themselves and their surroundings. We can teach teenagers to nurture positive emotions within themselves instead of feeling those negative outside influences.

When one young man was first starting to play sports competitively, he developed a pattern of negative thinking that he still struggles with. Even after a good game, the young man didn't feel good about his performance. He would constantly say that he could have scored more, passed better, found the open man, defended tighter, or been a better teammate.

The negative thoughts were worse after games that his team lost. After one particularly devastating defeat, this young man could be heard yelling at himself in a private corner of the locker room.

"You are horrible! Why did you even start playing basketball? You couldn't make a shot today. You're slow and selfish. Start passing the ball more! Stop taking stupid shots . . . "

The young man clearly thought he didn't play well, but his coach disagreed. Even though the team as a whole didn't play well that night, the young man had one of his better games, and the coach thought he shouldn't be verbally abusing himself. The coach went over to his player and started talking to him.

"You played great today. Your shot selection was great. What's got you down?" The player started talking, and the coach listened as the player meticulously told him, play by play, the things he didn't do right while neglecting all the things he did do right.

Listening was a great first step toward helping this young man nurture good emotions. Listening to teenagers shows that we care about them; however, we can do more than just listen. This young man, according to the perception of his coach, was a good ball player, but he thought otherwise. Perhaps he didn't even hear his coach compliment him on his playing because the negative thoughts were already occupying his mind. We need to find a way to help teenagers replace those negative thoughts.

One simple, practical way to help teenagers nurture good emotions about themselves is positive self-talk. A great example of this occurs in the YouTube video "Jessica's 'Daily Affirmation.'" A young child named Jessica stars in this adorable video by listing all the things she likes about life—from her parents to her pajamas. At the end, she exclaims, "I can do anything good!"[3] As silly as they may feel, teenagers can stand in front of a mirror just like Jessica and compliment themselves every day. Help them to see what they are doing right. It may be difficult for teenagers to do at first, so it may be helpful to provide them with a list of things that you admire about them to start with, and they can add to the list when they feel ready. Another technique is to encourage the use of a gratitude journal. Teenagers will be surprised with how much better they feel about themselves and their social acceptance as they foster an attitude of gratitude. People like to be around positive people. As teens learn to focus on the positives, they will attract more friends.

Keeping a Healthy Perspective

Teenagers can keep a healthy perspective by realizing that any perceived negative comments are just that person's opinion, and they don't need to let it affect them. Have you ever known a teenager who worked hard all summer and used some of that money to buy new clothes for school, only to go to school and hear someone tauntingly ask, "Where did you get *that* outfit?"

If that teen has a healthy perspective, he or she will say, "I like this outfit, and if you don't, that's your problem." If not, he or she may never wear those clothes again, no matter how much they cost.

When Brad speaks to teenagers, he asks them to raise their hands and vote on what they would do in the above situation. You guessed it. Virtually all of them say they would never wear that particular outfit again.

How can we help teenagers keep a healthy perspective? Teenagers need to realize that nother person's opinion is just that: one person's opinion. That feedback must always be weighed against your own opinion before decisions are made and judgment passed. As teenagers learn to focus on a healthy perspective, the opinions of friends, family members, and parents can also be weighed against one opinion of a friend or peer.

A healthy perspective sees mistakes as fixable and occasional bad days as OK. A healthy perspective sees the big picture and allows for hope amid trials. That kind of perspective makes it easier to reject friends who are bad influences and maintain friends who are uplifting.

As your hedgehog gets to know you by exploring, he develops positive signals, such as the feel and smell of your hands, that help him recognize you. Day after day, you will have an easier time picking up the hedgehog because the two of you have developed a friendship. A teenager develops friendships and views their own social acceptance much the same way as the hedgehog gets to know you—by exploring and developing positive signals. We can connect with teenagers by teaching them to **T-H-I-N-K** about friendships. As teenagers **try** new things, **help** others, **invest** in themselves, **nurture** positive emotions, and **keep** a healthy perspective, their perception of their own social acceptance will improve, and so will their self-esteem and circle of good friends.

Invitations to Action

How can you help teenagers develop a positive view of their social acceptance? These questions can help you T-H-I-N-K:

- What new skills and abilities did you develop as a teenager? How did that help you gain friends and improve your social acceptance?

- What are the benefits you have seen from serving and helping others? How can you help your teenager recognize those benefits in his or her life?

- What examples can you share with your teenager to encourage him or her to invest in developing talents?

- Think of a time when positive emotions and thoughts helped you endure a difficult situation. What lessons did you learn through that experience? How can you share that experience with your teenager? Are you modeling positive self-talk and expressing gratitude?

- How can you help teens keep negative comments of peers in perspective by giving more weight to their own opinions and the opinions of those who love them most? How can you help your teenager see the big picture?

Endnotes:

1. Meg Bostrom, "The 21st Century Teen: Public Perception and Teen Reality," Frameworks Institute (December 2001): 6.

2. Kathleen B. McElhaney, Jill Antonishak, and Joseph P. Allen. "They Like Me, They Like Me Not: Popularity and Adolescents' Perceptions of Acceptance Predicting Social Functioning Over Time." *Child Development* 79/3 (2008) 720.

3. "Jessica's 'Daily Affirmation,'" uploaded by dmchatster on YouTube, June 16, 2009. https://www.youtube.com/watch?v=qR3rKokZFkg.

Conclusion

"My Opinion Counts"

Remember our three rules for hugging a hedgehog?

1. Don't wear gloves; let him sniff you.

2. Take your time; let him relax. If he rolls into a ball and extends his quills, stay calm and be patient.

3. With both hands, scoop him up from the belly, which is covered with fur rather than quills. Let him explore you and become more comfortable with you.

We hope that the advice, stories, and information in this book have helped you learn that there are similarities between hugging a hedgehog and connecting with teens. No two hedgehogs are quite alike. No two teenagers are alike either. Each has differences that make him or her unique, but striving to implement general principles of communicating with them, helping them overcome adversity, and teaching them to develop a healthy self-esteem will help parents connect with their teenagers.

Wouldn't it be wonderful, though, if the hedgehog could tell us exactly how he wants to be held? We would no longer need to guess if we're holding him the right way; we could know for sure. Of course, that's not possible, but when it comes to connecting with teens, we have a valuable, yet underutilized resource—teenagers.

One young woman said, "I have something to say, even though I'm young. Adults seem to tune out teenagers because they think they aren't saying anything important. Even if that is the case, they are still saying something that's important to them."

Who better to talk to parents about helping young people than young people? When Brad was preparing a series of classes for parents on helping teenagers, he wanted teenage voices to be heard. He decided to share actual words and messages from young people. Brad conducted an informal survey of teenagers by distributing forms that said: "Tell your parents how you really feel." Over a thousand teenagers responded from all across North America.

Some comments were facetious, such as, "I wish they would give me a new car," or "They should let me stay out all night and not care," or "Hey, this is a switch—me giving my parents a lecture for a change! I sure hope they listen to me better than I listen to them!"

Funny comments aside, teenagers were excited about the possibility of giving their parents messages through that survey that some of them couldn't say in person. One of them commented, "It's neat that teenagers are finally going to have a say. I hope my comments can help." Another person wrote, "The words that we teenagers write on these little forms you have given us may not be profound like Socrates or Shakespeare, but they are profound in a different sense. They are profound in that they are sincere and coming straight from our hearts. The messages we write on these papers can help to shape, change, and mold relationships. I hope every parent will read these messages, and I hope they can make a difference."

Many expressed positive support and appreciation for parents. Some comments were extremely personal, like an anonymous one in which the teenager wrote a heartbreaking letter about divorce. Overall, the messages were well thought out, authentic, and insightful—even inspiring.

We know that to connect with teens, we must improve our communication with them, we must help them overcome adversity, and we must provide support as they build high self-esteem. But what do teenagers say about those subjects? While it's true that kids say the "darnedest" things, we would add that often they say the deepest things as well. The following comments from teens can deepen our understanding of exactly why, how, and in what ways teens want to connect with their parents. Here are just a few things that teens want us, as parents, to know:

"Communicate with Me"

Be more understanding. Take time to really listen to what I say and what I feel. Don't lecture all the time or get mad over small things. Don't interrupt when I talk. Remember that sometimes I just want to vent and not get advice. Talk openly and be straightforward and specific. Talk to me about sex and drugs. Offer me suggestions rather than giving me orders. Be quick to praise and slow to criticize.

When I am wrong, correct me when we're alone. I hate it when you lecture me in front of others. Be careful not to reveal my confidences to others in the family or in the community. Don't always say, "We know what it's like." I don't think you do. Being a teenager now is harder than you realize.

Respect me as a person. Tell me, "I love you." I like to hear it, and I need to hear it. Give me a hug, and don't be afraid to show you love me.

Spend more time together as a family, and don't watch so much TV and spend so much time on the computer. I understand that you have to work, but not all the time. Do more family activities, like going on a picnic or vacation or on special dates one-on-one. Get excited when I'm excited.

Show me you care about where I go and what I do. It hurts that you have stopped asking how things are going at school and with my friends. I want to talk about it if you will just listen and not judge.

"Help Me Overcome Trials"

Don't say that what is bothering me isn't important and that adults are the only ones with real problems. My problems are real to me. Don't yell at me. I have an "adult" in me that can be reasoned with. Be careful not to mock me, even when you say you are "just kidding."

There are a lot of temptations and problems facing teenagers today. I need to be able to talk about them openly, but it doesn't always have to be a serious matter. Let's lighten up a little and show a sense of humor.

I know you're busy and that others need time, but I'm important, too. Don't be afraid to set strict guidelines with me. I like knowing the boundaries, but be there to help me. Tell me why they matter.

Don't forget that I can change. Just because I did something stupid once doesn't mean I will do it again. Give me a chance to start over, and never give up on me—no matter what.

"Support Me as I Build My Self-Esteem"

Treat me like an adult instead of a little kid. Give me space to grow and make my own choices. Let me have some freedom; I won't abuse it. Trust me and don't just expect that I will do the wrong thing. I can make good choices if I'm given the chance.

Stop having a chip on your shoulder about teenagers. Let me have a say in what's happening. Just because you're older doesn't mean you are always right. My opinions count.

Please do not compare me to friends or my brothers and sisters. Treat us all equally and fairly. Playing favorites isn't good for anyone. Accept my individuality. I'm not exactly the same as others just because I'm in the same family. Be flexible.

Don't complain to your friends about me or tell others about my mistakes. I'm not perfect. I'm learning just like you. I make mistakes, but I can learn from them. Don't expect me to be perfect, and don't expect me to do something you're not willing to do yourself. Show you love me, even though you might sometimes be disappointed in what I do. Really care about me and my feelings.

Be with me because you like me, not just because it is your job. I might be more helpful if I were more appreciated. Notice what I do right, and tell me I'm great and worthwhile. I don't hear that enough.

"Just Try to Help Us See the Light"

At a youth gathering in southern California, Brad met a young man named Hector. During the conference, Brad gave him one of the survey forms and asked him to fill it out. He read the instructions and then said, "No, I can't do this."

"Come on," Brad encouraged him. "I would love to read what you have to say."

"No, I don't know what I'd write."

"Come on."

He was still hesitant. "There are lots of other teenagers here. You can find someone else."

Brad said, "I'll give surveys to them, too, but I really do want to know what you think. What is your message?"

He finally took the paper and said, "I don't really have anything to say, but I'll try."

At the concluding session of the conference, Brad was sitting toward the front of the room when someone tapped him on the shoulder and passed a folded note.

Brad unfolded the paper. It was a completed survey from Hector. As Brad read his words, he was touched deeply. This teenager who didn't have "anything to say" really said it all:

> *A teenage world is difficult,*
> *It's full of darkness, pain, and sin.*
> *There's pressure from both friends and foes*
> *Which causes confusion deep within.*
> *At times you want to get away*
> *And just be by yourself, alone.*

That's when you need your parents there
To calm your life when storms have blown.
Dear parents, please remember this:
For us each day is like a fight.
When teenagers are in the dark,
Just try to help us see the light.
—Hector Lopez

On the outside, teenagers may appear covered in quills and difficult to hug, but underneath those defenses, teenagers desperately want to be accepted, to be wanted, and to be loved. These teenagers that responded to Brad's survey have told us clearly what we should do to better connect with them. Communicate with your teenagers, help them overcome adversity, and support them as they build healthy self-esteem. It may take some time, but as you use these keys, you will be able to truly connect with your teens.

Appendix

Additional Sources

Some of the material in this book has been adapted from the following previously published books and articles:

Jones, Barbara Barrington and Brad Wilcox. *Straight Talk for Parents: What Teenagers Wish They Could Tell You.* Salt Lake City: Deseret Book, 1994.

Robbins, Jerrick. "It's OK to Cry." In *Lessons from my Parents: 100 Shared Moments that Changed Our Lives,* edited by Michelle Robbins, 247. Sanger, CA: Familius, 2013.

Wilcox, Brad and Jerrick Robbins. *The Best-Kept Secrets of Parenting: 18 Principles That Can Change Everything.* Sanger, CA: Familius, July 2014.

Wilcox, Brad. *Growing Up: Gospel Answers about Maturation and Sex.* Salt Lake City: Bookcraft, 2000.

———"May I Have This Dance?" *The New Era,* 9.7 (1979): 46–49.

About the Authors

BRAD WILCOX is an associate professor at Brigham Young University where he also works with such programs as Especially for Youth and Campus Education Week. He grew up in Ethiopia, Africa, and has also lived with his family in New Zealand and Chile. He is the best-selling author of many books, including *Tips for Tackling Teenage Troubles* and *Straight Talk for Parents: What Teenagers Wish They Could Tell You.* His children's picture book, *Hip, Hip, Hooray for Annie McRae!* was a top finalist for the children's choice award in Utah. He and his wife, Debi, have four children and five grandchildren.

JERRICK ROBBINS is the oldest of seven children and has his fair share of experiences that taught him the importance of strengthening the family. His short story, "It's OK to Cry," has been published in *Lessons from My Parents: 100 Shared Moments that Changed Our Lives.* He and his wife, Aimee, currently live in Utah. Jerrick and Brad co-authored *The Best-Kept Secrets of Parenting: 18 Principles That Can Change Everything.*

About Familius

Welcome to a place where mothers are celebrated, not compared. Where heart is at the center of our families, and family at the center of our homes. Where boo-boos are still kissed, cake beaters are still licked, and mistakes are still okay. Welcome to a place where books—and family—are beautiful. Familius: a book publisher dedicated to helping families be happy.

Visit Our Website: www.familius.com

Our website is a different kind of place. Get inspired, read articles, discover books, watch videos, connect with our family experts, download books and apps and audiobooks, and along the way, discover how values and happy family life go together.

Join Our Family

There are lots of ways to connect with us! Subscribe to our newsletters at www.familius.com to receive uplifting daily inspiration, essays from our Pater Familius, a free ebook every month, and the first word on special discounts and Familius news.

Become an Expert

Familius authors and other established writers interested in helping families be happy are invited to join our family and contribute online content. If you have something important to say on the family, join our expert community by applying at:

www.familius.com/apply-to-become-a-familius-expert

Get Bulk Discounts

If you feel a few friends and family might benefit from what you've read, let us know and we'll be happy to provide you with quantity discounts. Simply email us at specialorders@familius.com.

Website: www.familius.com

Facebook: www.facebook.com/paterfamilius

Twitter: @familiustalk, @paterfamilius1

Pinterest: www.pinterest.com/familius

The most important work

you ever do will be within the

walls of your own home.

FAMILIUS

CPSIA information can be obtained
at www.ICGtesting.com
Printed in the USA
LVHW040010050719
623185LV00001B/4